WITHDR

Efficiency, Stability, and Equity

EFFICIENCY, STABILITY, AND EQUITY

A Strategy for the Evolution of the Economic System of the European Community

A REPORT BY

Tommaso Padoa-Schioppa

with

Michael Emerson
Mervyn King
Jean-Claude Milleron
Jean Paelinck
Lucas Papademos
Alfredo Pastor
Fritz Scharpf

PREFACE BY

Jacques Delors

OXFORD UNIVERSITY PRESS
1987

338·914
P
CENTRAL

Oxford University Press, Walton Street, Oxford OX2 6DP

Oxford New York Toronto
Delhi Bombay Calcutta Madras Karachi
Kuala Lumpar Singapore Hong Kong Tokyo
Nairobi Dar es Salaam Cape Town
Melbourne Auckland

and associated companies in
Beirut Berlin Ibadan Nicosia

Oxford is a trade mark of Oxford University Press

Published in the United States
by Oxford University Press, New York

© *Commission of the European Communities, 1987*

All rights reserved. No part of this publication may be reproduced,
stored in a retrieval system, or transmitted, in any form or by any means,
electronic, mechanical, photocopying, recording, or otherwise, without
the prior permission of Oxford University Press

This book is sold subject to the condition that it shall not, by way
of trade or otherwise, be lent, re-sold, hired out or otherwise circulated
without the publisher's prior consent in any form of binding or cover
other than that in which it is published and without a similar condition
including this condition being imposed on the subsequent purchaser

British Library Cataloguing in Publication Data

Padoa-Schioppa, Tommaso
Efficiency, stability and equity: a report.
1. Europe Economic Community
I. Title II. Emerson, Michael
341.24'22 HC241.2
ISBN 0–19–828630–9
ISBN 0–19–828629–5 Pbk

Library of Congress Cataloguing in Publication Data

Data available

Set by H Charlesworth & Co Ltd, Huddersfield
Printed in Great Britain
at the University Printing House, Oxford
by David Stanford
Printer to the University

UNIVERSITY COLLEGE
LIBRARY
CARDIFF

Preface

There is no substitute for scientific investigation. It focuses attention on the balance that must exist between the different parts of a particular work. One of its inherent features is the attention to cohesion and unity.

The report entrusted by the European Commission to the small group of economists led by Tommaso Padoa-Schioppa is a scientific work. For all that, it does not lack commitment. Guided mainly by the principles of economic science, it sets about answering two questions of immediate relevance. What difficulties will be encountered between now and 1992 as we move towards completion of the Community-wide internal market? In what way should the workings of the Community be adapted in order to tackle those difficulties in the most effective manner?

The list of those difficulties will probably not cause any surprise among those with practical experience of constructing Europe. Allow me, however, to draw attention to the novel way in which the authors of the report have formulated their analyses, enabling us to see more clearly why certain 'natural' processes of economic integration have proved in practice to be so narrow:

● The principle of sectoral comparative advantage, which is often cited as the justification for the exchange of goods and services and for the gains this brings, is no longer, according to the authors, the only motor of commercial integration. The microeconomic complementarity between economies with closely related structures emerges as a no less decisive factor;

● The growing complexity of technical standardization and information networks is increasing the diversity of modern economies and is rendering extremely arduous, not to mention impossible, the task of harmonization in the strict sense of the term. It is becoming increasingly important to organize and plan for compatibility rather than to establish homogeneity;

● Because of the growing commercial interpenetration of our economies, national macroeconomic strategies are led towards a cautious bent. In the absence of other explicit and jointly agreed choices, such interpenetration may lead us in the direction of slower growth.

To put it another way, the 'invisible hand' that ensures the optimal allocation of factors, in a market characterized by the greatest possible freedom of supply and choice, is itself in need of guidance. This is probably the main lesson to be learnt from the analysis of the experts. While our sights are set on the internal market, a highly desirable objective in its own right, we must also take a broader view of things and display a wider-ranging ambition, extending the conscious scope of agreed policies beyond mere supervision of the orderly functioning of the market.

Hence the title of the report. The three values singled out, 'efficiency, stability, and equity', which are derived from the three celebrated functions identified by Musgrave, are a recurrent feature of the recommendations made.

Given the personality and experience of Tommaso Padoa-Schioppa, a patient propogator of monetary co-operation in Europe, it is not surprising that the report contains, in the first place, an appeal aimed at monetary policy-makers. The thrust of the appeal is clear. Full liberalization of capital movements will serve to weld financial markets in the Community closely together; it will also detract from the individual ability to control internal and external shocks. But to maintain the same degree of monetary stability as before, the co-ordination of national macroeconomic policies will have to be stepped up and the European monetary system reinforced.

Consequently, a more effective allocation of resources at Community level requires a strengthening of the capacity for policy management at this same level. Applying the logic of Musgrave, it also calls for a strengthening of the redistribution function. Since this is such a controversial matter, closer attention to it in the report would certainly have been welcome. Is it sufficient to increase the redistributive capacity of the Community budget, or must we also look at the quality of the transfers themselves, at their real economic effectiveness?

In practice, the question remains unanswered. However, the authors do shed some light on the matter through their judicious application of the 'principle of subsidiarity'. Tommaso Padoa-Schioppa and his group are right to remind us of this essential element that cements together federalist structures, namely the principle of transferring to a higher level only that which cannot be efficiently executed at a lower level. One could surely contest this or that particular application of the principle, but there will be general recognition of the importance of this point of political balance advocated by the authors of the report.

The regulation and distribution functions need to be strengthened at Community level. The success of the internal market depends on this, as does the economic and social equilibrium of the Community.

The new approach which the Commission has proposed in its document 'The Single Act: A New Frontier for Europe' corresponds to this vision. It consists neither of simple financial transfers nor of an excessive centralization of corrective measures. Rather it involves joint policies to complete or correct market forces, so creating a genuine common economic space, to be managed in a deliberate way, and with a view to the political union of Europe.

Tommaso Padoa-Schioppa and his colleagues thus provide us with a number of keys with which to face what seems to be the most pressing challenge facing our democracies as the twentieth century draws to a close, the challenge of diversity.

In this regard, they take care to remind us of the constraints of the Treaty and the Community: the balance between the costs and benefits of joint projects or measures is established within each country and in the economic sphere; and we know how this risks, at any time, being reduced to a mere matter of accounting.

Would the situation be different if defence or foreign policy or education were included among the public goods for which the Community is responsible? It is here that the historical comparisons made by the group assume their full significance. It is true that, in the past, particular political circumstances contributed to the establishment of certain small and large states, through the federation of their provinces. But is is also true that the mantle of political union — where necessary, imposed by force — served to obscure and consolidate profound inequalities in development, whose mechanisms exist still today.

And so, aware of our strengths and limitations, we need more than ever to understand exactly what kind of Europe we wish to construct.

Brussels
September 1987

Jacques Delors
President of the Commission
of the European Communities

Letter of Transmission

to Mr Jacques Delors
President
Commission of the European Communities

Dear President

In April 1986, the Commission decided to ask a Group of independent experts to investigate the economic consequences of the decisions taken in 1985 to enlarge the Community to include Spain and Portugal and to create a market without internal frontiers by the year 1992. The Group was invited to identify the problems that could arise in implementing these decisions and to suggest solutions.

In submitting the report of the Group to the Commission, I should like to briefly comment on three aspects of the work we have done: the analysis, the recommendations, the perspective.

At first sight, the two decisions of 1985 may not appear to have immediate 'systemic' implications, as they represent a geographical widening and an economic deepening of the common market project, which was the original objective of the Treaty of Rome. For several reasons, however, the implications are considerably more complex.

Through successive enlargements, the Community has become a much more heterogeneous area—in terms of economic structure, living standards, social systems, and policy institutions—than the original Community of six. Moreover, the market integration programme to be executed by 1992 covers the most difficult parts of the task originally set out by the Treaty of Rome, as it includes matters that have implications for personal freedom and security, monetary stability, and other politically sensitive issues. It is not by accident that such parts had been deferred for so many years.

In its analysis, the report shows how both the 1985 decisions affect the functioning of markets and prepare the ground for enormous improvements in the allocation of economic resources. Indeed, in 1992, the completion of an area of 320 million consumers and producers where goods, services, and factors of production circulate freely will represent a substantial advance—in terms of efficiency, welfare, and economic influence in the world—on the smaller 1985 market, segmented by innumerable internal barriers.

This progress, however, will have profound consequences for the two functions of policy that—in every economic system, including the Community—integrate policies and interact with them. These functions are the stabilization of the economy and the redistribution of income.

On the one hand, the complete liberalization of capital movements is

x	Letter of Transmission

inconsistent with the present combination of exchange rate stability and considerable national autonomy in the conduct of monetary policy; on the other hand, the complete opening of the market in the enlarged Community will have distributive effects that are likely to be stronger and more disruptive than those experienced in the sixties when trade integration proceeded among less heterogeneous countries and in a context of faster economic growth.

If these interactions between policies were neglected, or if the solutions chosen for them were inadequate, what in 1985 were rightly applauded as significant steps in the construction of Europe could encounter obstacles and entail inconsistencies. These could be erroneously taken as signs that the programme was mistaken, or too ambitious. The primary objective of a fully integrated internal market in an enlarged Community would lose political support and eventually fail, thereby depriving the Community of a major source of additional economic welfare.

It is therefore essential to design and implement, at this early stage of the 1986–92 process, the complementary programme needed to set the evolution of the Community on a balanced course.

In the view of the Group this requires a consistent strategy that would jointly address the three policy functions concerning market integration, stabilization of the economy and the equitable distribution of gains. Such a strategy represents a minimum, without which the success of the 'allocative programme', i.e. the completion of the internal market, would be jeopardized. This is the central proposition of the report.

The recommendations of the Group are based on this central proposition and can be summarized in the following points:

1. Implementation of the internal market programme within the deadline requires stronger reliance on the principle of mutual recognition of national regulations, a more selective choice of priority areas, less complex Community legislation, and effective solutions for the serious problem that is emerging with regard to compliance with Community law. In no circumstances should the 1992 deadline be shifted.

2. Monetary policy co-ordination and the mechanisms of the European Monetary System (EMS) will have to be significantly strengthened if freedom of capital movements and exchange rate discipline are to survive and coexist.

3. In a larger and more differentiated Community, redistributive functions performed through the budget and the lending instruments of the Community should be considerably developed in size and made more effective in their purpose and design.

4. Fourth, a stepping up in the growth rate observed in recent years will be necessary if the enlargement and the completion of the internal market are to be successful. This speed-up should result from both the market opening process and a 'co-operative growth strategy' such as has been proposed by the Commission to the Council.

To implement the recommendations of the report, and particularly those summarized in the first three points above, changes in the rules and working methods of the Community are required. To define such changes in detail was not the task of the Group. What clearly emerges from our work, however, is the scope for combining a gain in the effectiveness of Community action with greater decentralization of certain functions. The report shows how this principle of 'economic federalism', of which the mutual recognition of national regulations is an important example, can lead to effective and realistic solutions in many policy fields.

For each of the four sets of policy recommendations, specific actions are considered and suggested in the report.

I should like to add some remarks to place the report in perspective and to clarify its aims.

The report develops indications for several policy areas. The main point to stress, however, is the strength of the links between these areas. Too often interdependent issues are considered and negotiated separately, with the result that the overall equilibrium or disequilibrium associated with the chosen solutions is overlooked. Greater Community involvement in stabilization and redistribution policies is the indispensable complement of the ambitious project of completing the internal market: this is out first and most important proposition. Only if this proposition is accepted, will it be possible to agree on the specific action to be taken in each of the three policy areas.

In assessing the adequacy of the proposed strategy, it needs to be borne in mind that the Community's scope for economic action and successful development is, rather paradoxically, limited by the strictly economic nature of the Community itself. This is because the Community, unlike fuller political systems, is not responsible for the provision of essential 'public goods' such as defence, justice, and social security, with the important economic consequence that distributive issues become more acute owing to the need to balance costs and benefits for members in more narrow terms than in a complete political system. Consequently, the claim of a *juste retour* tends to be stronger than in other systems. Indeed, the budget of a strictly economic Community is both small and much concerned with distributive issues. As a further consequence, the support it can offer to economic activity and macroeconomic stabilization is barely significant.

From an economic point of view, if the re-emerging anxieties about European security gave rise to greater involvement of the Community in its own defence, then some of these economic problems could also be considerably eased.

The analysis and the recommendations of the report relate to a critical phase of the historical development of the Community. Since the creation of the European Monetary System in 1979, the evolution of the European Community has followed an agenda in which the efficient allocation of resources and the pursuit of price stability have ranked as the highest priorities. They are the priorities that the most successful economy in Europe has set for itself and proposed for the Community. The process of disinflation promoted by the EMS, the enlargement of the market to include new member countries, the programme for the complete dismantling of internal barriers and the movement towards complete capital liberalization are all items of this agenda. None of them could have been taken for granted ten years ago, when continued access to an open European market, which is the wide field on which the fruits of sound economic management are reaped, was in danger. The two decisions of 1985—confirmed by the Treaties of Accession and the Single European Act—mark the final acceptance of this agenda. The danger now comes from potentially disruptive imbalances between different policy dimensions in the Community. The success obtained by persuading the Community that efficient allocation of resouces and price stability come first is what today makes it necessary to verify the overall consistency of the Community's design for the years to come.

The report does not deal with conjunctural matters, but it deals with urgent matters. It almost exclusively discusses systemic problems, and it offers solutions that have an unavoidable institutional content. These solutions cannot be postponed, but need to be implemented early in the period set for the completion of the internal market.

Tommaso Padoa-Schioppa
Chairman of the Group

Brussels
April9l 87

Contents

Contents

PART D: TOWARDS A BALANCED DEVELOPMENT OF THE
COMMUNITY SYSTEM

Annexes

Composition of the Group

Chairman
TOMMASO PADOA-SCHIOPPA

Members
PROFESSOR MERVYN KING

PROFESSOR JEAN PAELINCK

PROFESSOR LUCAS PAPADEMOS

PROFESSOR ALFREDO PASTOR

PROFESSOR FRITZ SCHARPF

Rapporteur
MICHAEL EMERSON,

Jean-Claude Milleron contributed as a member of the Group to the preparation of the report, but did not share in all the final conclusions.

The group met five times between September 1986 and February 1987, in Brussels, London, and Paris. Some members of the Group held hearings in Athens, Dublin, Lisbon, and Madrid in the course of February 1987. Professor Paul Krugman of the Massachusetts Institute of Technology presented a paper to one of the Group's meetings, and this is published as Annex A to the present report. The Group also benefited from helpful suggestions from Professor Alexis Jacquemin of the University of Louvain-la-Neuve; Professor Jean-Victor Louis of the Free University of Brussels; Dr Jacques Pelkmans of the European Institute of Public Administration, Maastricht; Professor Luigi Spaventa of the University of Rome; and Professor Joseph Weiler of the European University Institute, Florence. Research assistance was provided by M. Vanheukelen, J. Van Ginderachter, F. Ilzkovitz, and J. McKenna; with secretarial and administrative support from Alison Molders and Chantal Mathieu.

All members of the Group have participated in a personal capacity, and views expressed in the report are not to be attributed to the various organizations with which they are associated.

The report was submitted to the Commission of the European Communities on 10 April 1987.

Tommaso Padoa-Schioppa, Italian, is Deputy Director General of the Banca d'Italia. He graduated in economics from Bocconi University, Milan and the Massachusetts Institute of Technology. His earlier career included working as an economist in the Research Department of the Banca d'Italia, and was from 1979 to 1983 Director-General for Economic and Financial Affairs at the Commission of the European Communities in Brussels.

Michael Emerson, British, is Director for the Economic Evaluation of Community Policies at the Commission of the European Communities in Brussels. He graduated in Politics, Philosophy and Economics at Balliol College, Oxford. Earlier positions included working as an economist at the Organisation for Economic Cooperation and Development in Paris. In 1985–1986 he was Fellow, Centre for International Affairs, Harvard University.

Mervyn King, British, is Professor of Economics at the London School of Economics. He graduated in economics at King's College, Cambridge. Earlier positions included teaching at Cambridge University, Harvard University, University of Birmingham, and at the Massachusetts Institute of Technology. His writings include books and numerous articles on the economics of taxation.

Jean-Claude Milleron, French, is Directeur de la Prévision at the Ministry of Finance in Paris. He is a graduate of the Ecole Polytechnique and has a degree in economic sciences from the University of Paris. His career has included positions as administrator at INSEE and director of ENSAE. He is currently Chairman of the Economic Policy Committee of the European Communities.

Jean Paelinck, Belgian, is Professor of Theoretical Spatial Economics at the Erasmus University, Rotterdam, and Director of the Netherlands Economic Institute. He graduated in economics and law at the University of Liège and has lectured at universities in France, Belgium, England, Canada, the United States, Poland, Venezuela and Colombia. He is the author of numerous books and articles on spatial economics and econometrics.

Lucas Papademos, Greek, is economic adviser to the Governor of the Bank of Greece. He studied and received a doctorate in economics at the Massachusetts Institute of Technology, and has taught at Columbia University and the Athens Graduate School of Economics. He has written extensively on macroeconomic and monetary policy, and is currently a member of the Monetary Committee of the European Communities.

Alfredo Pastor, Spanish, is President of a public utility in Barcelona (Empresa Nacional Hidro-electrica de Ribagorzana). He graduated in economics at the University of Barcelona and received a doctorate at the Massachusetts Institute of Technology. He has taught economics at the Universities of Barcelona and Boston, and has worked at the World Bank and, as Vice-President, at the Instituto Nacional de Industria, Madrid.

Fritz Scharpf, German, is Director of the Max-Planck-Institut für Gesellschaftsforschung in Cologne. He received law degrees from the University of Freiburg and Yale Law School. He has taught law and political science at Yale and Chicago Law Schools and at the University of Constance. From 1973 to 1984 he was Director of the International Institute of Management at the Science Center, Berlin. He is author of numerous articles and books.

1
Introduction

The Group was asked to review the Community's strategy for further economic integration in the light of recent developments. These include the decision taken by the European Council in 1985 to complete the internal market by 1992, and the third enlargement bringing in Portugal and Spain in 1986.

In announcing the beginning of this project, the Commission noted [40]:

These recent developments will generate many interactions in the Community's system of policies and institutions. For example, capital market liberalisation will affect the European Monetary System and the needs for macroeconomic policy coordination. The opening of goods, service and factor markets may also be expected to have important impacts at the regional and sectoral level. In general terms, there arises the question of the desirable degree of parallelism in the development of different common policies, such that the 'Community system' as a whole progresses in a balanced way.

The report is divided into four parts:

Part A is a general summary of the report.

Part B sets out a few theoretical propositions that are of central importance to our report. Some historical experiences are also recalled.

Part C reviews the Community system as it is functioning and developing at the present time. The main features of the internal market programme— for goods, services, labour and capital—are evaluated, followed by a short review of macroeconomic policy co-ordination questions and the Community budget.

Part D takes a forward look. After summarizing the problems and interactions posed by the completion of the internal market in an enlarged Community, ideas are presented for a harmonious and efficient development of the Community system. This prescriptive part of the report is structured around the familiar distinction made in the economic analysis of public policy between three main branches: resource allocation, macroeconomic stabilization, and redistribution for reasons of equity.

For the busy reader, Part A and Chapters 3 and 10 amount to a self-contained summary of the report. For the reader with a little more time, the whole of Parts B and D are the next most important.

PART A
SUMMARY

A Strategy for the Evolution of the European Community

The Group was asked to assess the implications for the economic system of the Community of recent decisions: adoption of the internal market programme, and the latest enlargement bringing in Spain and Portugal.

Our review leads to the conclusion that there are indeed important linkages between these initiatives and other strategic aspects of the Community system. These linkages pose requirements for other Community policies if the internal market programme is to have a good chance of success, and if the Community's economic and political integration is to proceed in a politically and economically viable way.

2.1 Four main points

The main argument may be summarized under four points:

1. The 1985 White Paper [1] on the internal market implies a very strong action to improve the *efficiency of resource allocation* in the Community. The Group strongly supports the final objective and the 1992 target date for its completion. But the programme is getting behind schedule. The most difficult parts are not yet tackled. There are some aspects of the programme where flexibility will be required to permit changes in method and emphasis.

2. The internal market programme creates both opportunities and needs for complementary action to foster the Community's macroeconomic stability and growth. As regards *monetary stability*, the elimination of capital controls, coupled to the requirement of exchange rate stability, means a qualitative change in the operating environment for monetary policy. It will require moving closer to unification of monetary policy. In a quite fundamental way, capital mobility and exchange rate fixity together leave no room for independent monetary policies. In these conditions, it is pertinent to consider afresh the case for a strengthened organization of monetary co-ordination or institutional advances in this field. Advantages for stabilization policy can justify such changes.

3. There are serious risks of aggravated *regional imbalance* in the course of market liberalization. This is because different economic processes will be at work as markets integrate, some tending towards convergence, others towards divergence. Neither dogmatic optimism nor fatalistic pessimism is warranted in these respects. Opportunities for convergence will be increased, but adequate accompanying measures are required to speed adjustment in the

structurally weak regions and countries, and counter tendencies towards divergence. In addition, reforms and development of Community structural funds are needed for this purpose—alongside other reforms for the Community budget as regards agricultural spending and its financing.

4. As for *growth*, the internal market programme, if successful, must mean a perceptible increase in the rate of macroeconomic expansion. There is no way major benefits could be supposed to accrue without this. Indeed, without generating higher growth, the political cost of negotiation would hardly be worthwhile and the programme would fail. The conversion of better functioning markets into macroeconomic results cannot be taken for granted. This does not mean, however, a call for a burst of short-term demand expansion. On the other hand, something along the lines of the Community's co-operative growth strategy [36, 37] must be translated from declarations of principle into reality.

These four points may be regrouped logically in the following way. In terms of overall strategy, the Community has in recent years adopted a clear-cut economic agenda—characterized by the pursuit of (*a*) *competitive markets* and (*b*) *monetary stability*. There is increasing consensus over the fundamental wisdom of these choices. They assure, on the one hand, the efficiency of resource allocation and, on the other hand, a vital sustainability condition for economic policy. This agenda is, however, incomplete. Two further elements must be added: (*c*) an equitable *distribution* of the gains in economic welfare, and (*d*) actual *growth* performance. Neither of them are adequately assured as of now. Without them, the Community's system would be likely to falter. A successful strategy will therefore require also adequate mechanisms to aid structural change in the regions and avoid distributive inequities and a preparedness to support the growth process through macroeconomic policy.

Agreement on these four points together should, in the Group's judgement, be the basis of the long-term 'social contract' between the Community and all its Member States. The essential interdependence between these features of integrated economic systems is well founded in economic theory (Chapter 3) and supported by historical experiences (Chapter 4).

We now spell out our conclusions in a little more detail.

2.2 Appraisal of the Community system to date

Goods and services markets

Chapter 5. Empirical and theoretical research in economics support the view that large economic gains have been made by the Community as a result of its market opening measures, especially among the six original member countries. Correspondingly, large economic gains could again be made by the Community with a programme of full integration of the internal market in an enlarged group of twelve countries.

However, since about 1973, trade integration among the original six members has large stagnated, as new market barriers outweighed new liberalizing action, and economic growth was halved. These events were significantly related, even if other factors also contributed in slowing down growth. Some of the main trade barriers are as follows. Important border taxes or national production or trade quotes have been reintroduced in agriculture, steel and textiles. The number of contestable national subsidy schemes has greatly increased. Government procurement restrictions, covering almost one-tenth of the economy, have hardly been eased at all. Attempts to harmonize technical standards at the Community level were becoming increasingly frustrated until use of the principle of mutual recognition of national regulations began to open fresh prospects. Civil aviation remains a highly uncompetitive market, and progress in this area, so far very slight, is highly desirable for reasons of commerce and the people's Europe. Financial services are still heavily protected—generally in insurance, and in several countries as regards banking.

The general introduction of the value-added tax was an important tax reform, helpful for undistorted resource allocation. However, the task of abolishing fiscal frontiers remains.

Labour markets

Chapter 6. Labour market mobility is assured (or will be in a few years for the new Members) from a legal point of view, but much remains to be done to establish truly open and competitive markets in many professions. On the other hand, the Community should be cautious about venturing further into the fields of labour market or social security harmonization because there needs to remain scope for national policy experimentation and adjustments.

Capital markets

Chapter 7. Considerable progress is now being made in capital market liberalization, although unevenly between countries. The removal of capital controls increases the need for associated actions to harmonize regulatory requirements and regimes for the taxation of capital income. It will also profoundly affect monetary and exchange rate policies, as indicated further below.

Macroeconomic policy

Chapter 8. The European Monetary System has effectively promoted a convergence on monetary stability. However, there should not be self-satisfaction with the status quo. The institutional fragility of the system will need to be rectified, notably with the opening of capital markets. Moreover, the system for co-ordination of budgetary and other policies under the 1974 Convergence Decision has been ineffective.

Community budget

Chapter 9. The expenditure functions of the budget (agriculture, regional, retraining, industrial, and aid policies) were in principle well chosen. But failure to control agricultural spending, apart from being very costly in itself, has led to problems of 'tokenism' in some other Community policies (i.e. contributions towards policy objectives which are too small to be significant), and friction in relation to financial costs and trade policy.

2.3 For a balanced development of the Community system

Rethinking the system

Chapter 10. This review of the system shows a mixed pattern of achievement and regress, of innovation and stagnation. The most promising development, the EMS and the internal market programme, do not at present add up to a balanced strategy for the evolution of the Community system as a whole. In fact, they contain inconsistencies. In the pursuit of a systematic rather than *ad hoc* approach, the Group uses the distinction between the allocation, stabilization, and distribution branches of public policy. The Group judges that the Community's important initiative in the allocation branch (through the internal market programme) needs to be balanced by development also in the stabilization and distribution branches. Such balance is required not to enlarge the competences of the Community for its own sake, but to ensure the success of the allocative programme.

The internal market and the allocation function

Chapter 11. With the three hundred or more items of legislation envisaged to complete the internal market by 1992, it is important that the Community intensify its search for methods of action that will minimize problems of implementing Community legislation in the Member States, and thereby also reduce compliance problems. In this context, the Group strongly welcomes the introduction of the mutual recognition principle to lower costs of harmonization, and feels that this principle can be extended further by taking a more positive view of 'competition among rules'. This is one of several respects in which we favour positive decentralization measures, to balance politically in some degree the centralization of powers implied by the White Paper. Recent trends point to the emergence of serious and growing compliance problems, and this calls for systemic reforms in the direction of greater decentralization of Community policies.

Effective competition policy and discipline over certain types of state subsidies will become more important for the Community with the completion of the internal market. A Community capacity to police mergers becomes more relevant. Major economic benefits from the opening of markets depend upon private sector confidence in the solidity of Community disciplines over state subsidies that sharply affect competitive conditions; without such confidence, enterprises will be hesitant to adopt Community market strategies. However, decentralization measures should also be considered here, for example through raising threshold sizes below which national subsidy schemes are excluded from or subjected less to Community surveillance. Steps should also be taken to facilitate private litigation in national courts in support of Community competition policy, and so relieve enforcement bottlenecks in the Community institutions.

Collaborative industrial ventures and policies will not always threaten the advantages of competition policy. Instances may be found where companies in third countries risk gaining world monopoly or oligopoly situations. Within the Community, it may only be possible to eliminate some restraints (such as in government procurement) by restructuring industries with cross-frontier regroupings of companies. In some cases, this could in turn be facilitated by the privatization of companies producing tradeable goods.

A new approach to corporation tax harmonization is suggested, with a view to removing fiscal distortions for European enterprises and capital.

Capital mobility, the EMS and the stabilization function

Chapter 12. Capital market liberalization will fundamentally change the environment for monetary policy in a fixed (or nearly fixed) exchange rate system such as the EMS. Domestic monetary policies have to be much more nearly unified, which raises crucial questions about how co-ordination is organized or institutionalized.

With complete capital mobility, the present mechanisms of the EMS and the existing weak degree of monetary policy co-ordination will no longer be sufficient to foster price stability and to ensure orderly trade relationships in the Community. Institutionalizing greater exchange rate flexibility would be an inadequate and potentially dangerous answer to the problems posed by capital mobility. Stronger EMS mechanisms coupled with strengthened monetary co-ordination is the course to be followed if the basic performance of the EMS is to be preserved.

The Group identifies the characteristics of a 'Stage Two' EMS that could reconcile capital mobility and a high degree of exchange rate fixity: (*a*) stronger co-ordination and joint management of monetary policy; (*b*) strengthened EMS mechanisms to counter speculative capital movements; (*c*) a new model of safeguard mechanisms, providing for more effective Community control over exceptional derogations from complete capital mobility; and (*d*) well-structured Community participation in international monetary co-operation.

These developments would also require a reconsideration of the roles of the relevant Community bodies (the Monetary Committee and the Committee of Governors), and a more developed role for the ECU, with links between its presently separate private and official markets.

The 'Stage Two' would not amount to a monetary union. Indeed, while recognizing that a monetary union has several first-best properties from an economic point of view, the Group does not advocate a precipitous move in this direction. There would have to be further adaptation of attitudes and behaviour among private agents (employers and trade unions), as well as of political attitudes, for monetary union to be a sufficiently low-risk proposition.

As monetary integration progresses, national budgets will also have to be subject to intenser common disciplines. However, the decentralized model evident in the mature federations, where the capital market exerts some restraint on state borrowing, is more plausible in the long run than power-sharing arrangements that have sometimes been considered.

The Community budget and the distribution function

Chapter 13. Just as capital market liberalization will drastically affect the operating environment for monetary policy in the EMS, so also a triple challenge in the 'real' economy is going to intensify the need for an adequate regional policy in the Community. This triple challenge consists of the internal market programme, the enlargement of the Community to include more diverse economies, and new trends in industrial technologies. Any easy extrapolation of 'invisible hand' ideas into the real world of regional economics in the process of market-opening measures would be unwarranted in the light of economic history and theory. In addition, current trends in industrial structure in favour of high technology industries point on the whole to an aggravation of the problems of backward and peripheral regions, and, sometimes, of old declining industrial regions.

The Single European Act, in Article 130A to E, rightly suggests a wide conception of how the Community should assure its 'economic and social cohesion'. The structural funds of the Community budget represent only one of several instruments for pursuing this objective. Consistency of macro- and microeconomic policies with the market-opening strategy of the Community is of the greatest importance. Also relevant are Community policies towards state subsidies, the stimulation of industrial R&D and the management of quota regimes for various industrial and agricultural products: all should give due attention to the regional aspect.

As regards the structural funds, the Group supports a substantial increase in their size and their proposed concentration on two types of regional problem: (*a*) the less-favoured and often peripheral regions, and (*b*) the old industrial regions suffering from economic decline. The structural funds should offer incentives to these categories of regions to build up or restore high levels of physical and human capital endowment, such that a faster growth of output and employment could be sustained. An increasing reliance on the programme-financing approach is advocated: this can function in a largely decentralized manner. Where budgetary transfers to low-income member countries become quite substantial in macroeconomic terms, they should be associated with agreement over medium-term macroeconomic policy strategy between the Community and the country concerned.

The agricultural budget has increasingly developed into an instrument of income redistribution rather than of stabilizing prices and incomes along trend paths that would be consistent with efficient resource allocation. This reversal of roles, from allocation to distribution, is highly unsuitable for the Community. Income maintenance functions are best discharged at lower levels of government. This would imply re-establishing a proper agricultural resource allocation policy at the Community level, and integrating the distribution function more into national income maintenance systems, subject to conditions, controlled by the Community, that separated such income support from production aids. There should be corresponding changes in the mechanisms and control of agricultural policy.

For the funding of the Community budget, it is important to support the institutional principle of 'own resources'. From a distributive point of view, the main revenue sources, beyond customs duties and agricultural levies, should be either neutral or progressive with respect to national income. Together with the other budgetary reforms recommended, there should be a much reduced need for *ad hoc* budget compensation mechanisms, whose negotiation has been very costly politically in the past. However, the group envisages a safeguard mechanism designed to settle problems of budgetary inequity in a systematic and permanent way. As a result, political negotiations over 'allocative' policies should be more concentrated on efficiency considerations and divorced from 'distributive' considerations.

Growth conditions

Chapter 14. It is necessary to stress the need for consistent micro- and macroeconomic strategies in the Community. The internal market programme can deliver valuable benefits in terms of a higher rate of economic growth, and indeed can deliver no real benefits except in this way. Macroeconomic policy must be geared towards supporting the emergence of such a higher growth rate. Economic growth has recently been about 2.5 per cent per annum, whereas the Community's co-operative growth strategy envisages a 3.5 per cent growth until the beginning of the next decade. With vigorous implementation of the internal market programme, the growth rate could even be further raised, possibly to 4.0 per cent for a period of years (in the

1960s, the rate of growth in the Community was 4.8 per cent). A sustained impetus on both supply and demand sides is needed to get an acceleration of growth clearly underway. In this way, many of the protectionist instincts impeding agreement on the internal market programme could be overcome. Without it the programme as a whole would be implausible.

2.4 Institutional issues

Finally, we regroup some of the conclusions in terms of institutional issues. In this respect, three headings appear to sum up the conditions for a viable evolution of the Community system:

1. *More selectivity in Community responsibilities.* The Group feels that the Community's effectiveness is undermined by expectations that it contributes to an excessively wide range of policy domains. There are sound principles to govern the selection of priority tasks for the Community. They are those of subsidiarity (the Community only does what it can do better than the nations), and the importance of cross-frontier spill-overs in the impact of given policies. There are a few priority areas where the Community's powers or institutions need to be strengthened or reformed. These concern monetary policy, regional policy, and policies to strengthen the competitivity of European enterprise. There are other areas where the Community's expected role, at least for harmonizing legislation, could be lessened: for example, social policy and labour market regulations.

2. *More space for decentralized application of Community policies.* Within its main areas of responsibility, the Community should prefer techniques of policy-making that allow for decentralized implementation in the details. The Community needs to confirm its recent moves away from conceptions of monolithic harmonization, with Community competences replacing national competences, towards a pluralistic, pragmatic, and federalistic model in which national policies and legislation are framed within wider Community rules. This will mean, in general terms, more shared policies, rather than the wholesale transfer of policies from national to Community levels of compe-tence. Some examples of the mechanisms that could work in these directions are: (*a*) maximum use of the mutual recognition principle, in the field of harmonization; (*b*) the programme-financing approach to management of the structural funds; (*c*) higher threshold levels exempting subsidies from Commu-nity jurisdiction; (*d*) more scope for national income maintenance measures in the agricultural sector; (*e*) executive responsibilities for Community policies shared in some cases through the work of management committees of the Commission and Member States; (*f*) maximum decentralized choice of indirect tax rates within the context of abolishing fiscal frontiers; and (*g*) a rethinking of strategies for tackling the growing problem of non-compliance with Community law.

3. *Stronger institutional powers in some priority areas.* Set against this background

of greater selectivity and preference for decentralized techniques of policy management, it becomes more realistic politically to make advances in the Community's institutional capacities in some priority domains. Thus, in the monetary area it is necessary to move towards a European central banking system with considerably enhanced policy co-ordination and executive responsibilities. In the field of competition policy, it is necessary to provide for reinforced capacity to control the most important infringements. In the field of the Community budget, there should be reforms with a view to better controlling agricultural expenditure, for example through mechanisms that automatically revise intervention commitments when expenditures risk overshooting budgeted amounts. In the domain of the structural funds, the Commission should have greater scope to accept or decline the co-financing of eligible programmes on the basis of quality control criteria, and, in certain cases, macroeconomic criteria.

PART B
THE SCHEMA OF IDEAS

3
Some Theoretical Propositions and Concepts

Although this report is not of a theoretical nature, there are certain concepts that need to be set out clearly from the beginning, since these will be referred to recurrently.

Four propositions, with solid foundations in economic theory and applied analysis, are of central importance to this study.

1. *There are great economic benefits to be obtained from increased openness to trade in goods and services among countries.* Such benefits have long been recognized to be available to countries which trade on the basis of different comparative advantages. More recently, however, trade theory has shown that great benefits can also flow from trade integration among countries with similar economic structures. Trade in the Community is largely of this second type. Detailed case studies show the gains from this second category of trade to be of very high orders of magnitude. These gains materialize in terms of lower prices for goods and services, higher quality, and wider consumer choice. The mobility of factors of production (capital and labour) also offers economic advantages, albeit on certain conditions for monetary and budgetary policies. Overall, therefore, economic analysis amply supports the intuition behind the Community's programme to complete the internal market, namely that this political initiative could deliver economic benefits of strategic importance.

2. The second category of gains from trade just mentioned derive from the fact that many industries can often continue to exploit economies of scale where the structure of companies concerned is becoming oligopolistic, even in an economic region as large as the Community. These are industries with important fixed costs, in which increasing returns to scale lead to the increasing specialization of enterprises. This means, however, that *the risks of an uneven distribution of the gains from trade on the one hand and of transitional employment problems on the other are serious*, and that several types of complementary policies require serious attention: competition policy including strong restraints on industrial policies at the level of individual countries, and policies to help even out the gains in the process of trade rationalization and expansion. This is relevant to the decision of Member States, set out in the Single European Act, to consider what steps may have to accompany the market-opening process in order to maintain the cohesion of the Community.

3. Alongside the accumulation of microeconomic efficiency gains as a result of increased economic interdependence, there is also the build-up of risks for the conduct of national macroeconomic policies. The most probable risk in

the event of increasing economic interdependence is that of excessive disinflation in macroeconomic policy management and thus an aggravation of employment problems. These risks have to be countered by improved co-ordination of macroeconomic policies, otherwise the microeconomic gains may be significantly offset by macroeconomic losses. *The microeconomic efficiency gains from market integration have to be associated with a higher rate of macroeconomic growth, otherwise there is no gain for the economy as a whole.* In other words, the reallocation of resources will only be beneficial if the resources freed by rationalization are actually re-employed.

4. Where the market-opening process includes the complete liberalization of capital movements, there is a qualitative change in the operating environment for macroeconomic policy, and monetary policy in particular. Under these conditions, countries which wish at the same time to share stable exchange rates must co-ordinate their monetary policies to an extremely high degree, otherwise the system will fail. (The reasons why this is the case are set out in 12.1 and Annex A below). *Thus, seeking to maintain open capital markets, stable exchange rates, and autonomous macroeconomic policies is fundamentally inconsistent.* In considering how to satisfy this requirement for a high degree of monetary policy co-ordination, it may in several respects be more efficient to move beyond co-ordination towards the unification of monetary policies. This has institutional implications, and raises other problems that need to be considered.

These four central propositions call for a fuller justification, and this is provided in appropriate sections of the report. An account of how these points relate more precisely to current economic thinking is given in Annex A, which also gives references to the literature.

Taken together, these propositions draw attention to the strong linkages that exist between different parts of the Community system. This emphasizes also the need for a unifying conceptual framework to help assess the desirable structure and evolution of the system. Such a framework is offered by two elements: (*a*) the economic principles of multi-tier government, and (*b*) the well-known primary breakdown of the functions of public policy between the allocation, stabilization, and distribution branches.

As regards the first element, in the Community there are often four levels of government to be considered: local, regional, national, and Community. The essential criterion for assessing the most efficient level of government for a given policy function is the incidence of the costs and benefits of the policy action [2]. The most suitable level of government to provide a given public good is in principle that which encompasses the larger part of these costs and benefits. *The right level of government is then the lowest level at which the function in question can be efficiently executed. This is called the 'principle of subsidiarity',* because it states that higher levels of government should only exert functions that cannot be efficiently performed at lower levels. However, where significant fractions of the costs and benefits spill over beyond the jurisdiction of the government in question, there is likely to be an inefficiency in policy-making: undersupply of public goods where the benefits spill over, oversupply where the costs spill over. One type of action to correct such bias is through co-ordination between governments, and another is through systems of budget-ary transfers between levels of government. However, the problems of spill-overs may be too great for these mechanisms to handle adequately, in which case the transfer of competences to a higher level of government is the more radical solution.

The second element of the conceptual framework is the well-known *primary breakdown of the functions of public policy between three branches* [3]. While far from completely separate in practice, the distinction is nonetheless useful for the purposes of exposition. The three branches are:

1. The resource *allocation function*, which is concerned mainly with microeco-nomic policy instruments aimed at the efficient use of resources.

2. The *stabilization function*, which is concerned with the macroeconomic policy objectives of high standards of price stability and high levels of economic activity and employment.

3. The income *redistribution function*, which can have many dimensions including, for example, inter-personal and inter-regional aspects.

The Community, at its beginning and now again with emphasis on the completion of the internal market, has been given some important compe-tences in the resource allocation function. This is in line with the view that only a large region can deliver the potential benefits of the market economy.

The stabilization function has long been regarded as being at the heart of national level macroeconomic policy-making. However, as already pointed out, with increasing interdependence between countries through the opening of markets, the workings of national macroeconomic policy suffer from increased spill-overs between countries. With the addition of capital market liberalization, these effects of national policy actions on other countries become very important. Therefore, the stabilization function becomes natur-ally drawn upwards also in the systemic organization of policies.

The redistribution function is first of all a matter of policies affecting inter-personal income distribution through tax and social security systems, and the distribution between capital and labour incomes. These are policies which so far in the Community have had rather limited spill-over effects between countries. Therefore the case for Community involvement is weak. However, the market-opening policies of the Community create distributional issues because there is no a priori certainty that the aggregate gains from these policies will translate into gains for all participants at the level of regions or countries. The Community needs to give, accordingly, due attention to these aspects of the distribution function.

Thus the Community's economic system, which has been led by policy functions affecting resource allocation, is having increasingly diffuse implications for the other main branches of public policy. *A certain balance or degree of parallelism in the evolution of the Community's responsibilities under each of three main branches of the public policy system is required if the integration process is to prove viable and robust.*

This structure of ideas is used in more detail in Part D of this report, which sets out our views for a balanced development of the system.

4
Historical Experiences

While the following few pages will surely appear excessively simple to historians, there are none the less some important messages from earlier historical experiences which need to be remembered. In particular, it is suggested that the theoretical points made above have also loomed large in the practical history of nations. Three categories of experiences are identified: those relating to (1) economic integration, (2) monetary unions and systems, and (3) to differences between economic and political communities.

1. Economic integration. The history of economic integration suggests that the aggregate welfare gains of market openness are very large, but that the even distribution of these gains cannot be taken for granted. History is replete with examples of regional conflicts over the terms of trade or degrees of protection for industrial and agricultural produce, between north and south geographical divides, and between the interest of initially more versus less advanced economies. There is abundant evidence that those embarking upon the course of economic integration should not rely on simple beliefs about the benevolence of 'invisible hands'. A few examples illustrate this.

In Germany, following establishment of the Zollverein in 1834, the industrially more advanced Prussia and Saxony increased their market shares in Southern Germany at the expense of British and French competitors, while the south obtained some compensating advantage for its agriculture. Historians now tend to the view that industrial development in the south was retarded by the customs union. That the effect was not more damaging is ascribed to the vigorous industrialization policies followed by some of the southern states, for which they retained full autonomy, with the exception of a common external tariff and, later, a common currency [4].

In Italy, unification was associated with the lowering of protective tariffs for industry in the south and a general lowering in the level of agricultural protection. In spite of the promotion of major railway investments in the south, industry there was unable to withstand the competition from the north; agriculture in the south, with rigid land-holding and social customs, also proved incapable of withstanding competition from the north of Italy and other efficient producers north of the Alps. The widely held view is that the economy of the south suffered rather than benefited for decades after unification.

In the United States, after the Revolution, the conflict of interest between the industrializing north and the agricultural south, whose economy relied heavily upon slave labour, was endemic. The north pushed for higher tariffs for industrial commodities; when, in alliance with the new western states, they succeeded in this, the south resorted to the nullification of interstate treaties, and eventually to secession. After losing the consequent Civil War, the south lapsed into a century of economic stagnation from which it has only recently emerged with migration of northern industry to the sun-belt states [5].

2. Monetary unions and systems. European history of the last century also offers several case-studies in regional monetary unions [6].

France was the initiating force behind the Treaty of 1865 forming the Latin monetary union with Italy, Belgium, and Switzerland. The Treaty agreed that all countries would mint only coins of common weight, fineness, diameter, and so on, which would be mutually acceptable to their respective treasuries. Greece also joined, and with further bilateral treaties or unilateral actions as many as eighteen states had by 1880 adopted the French monetary unit as the basis of the national systems. The union then effectively lapsed as silver coinage, the basis to the system, had to be suspended because of its loss of value in relation to gold. More fundamentally, however, the union lacked any mechanism enabling the countries to consult and agree on co-ordinated actions.

A Germanic monetary union was formed in 1857 with a treaty between Austria and the members of the Zollverein. It dissolved, however, with the war in 1866 between Prussia and Austria. A Scandinavian monetary union was created in 1873 by Denmark, Sweden and Norway, each country producing standard gold coins but retaining the right of issuing subsidiary coinage and notes convertible into gold. The Scandinavian union also established a clearing system for coin and notes, and succeeded in economizing in gold and becoming technically considerably more advanced than the Latin union. The success of the Scandinavian system tends to be attributed to the structural similarity of the three participating economies. But its demise during the first World War is attributed to the lack of a sufficiently strong managing authority to handle the serious international monetary problems caused by the war.

The gold standard was a unique system characterized by an automatic rule governing balance of payments adjustments and the determination of the world price level [7, 8, 9]. From about 1876 to 1913, all the major industrial powers, including the United States, were operating under the rules of the gold standard, with London serving as financial centre of the system. These countries thus gave up independence in monetary policy in favour of free trade, free capital mobility and fixed exchange rates. Fiscal policies were not a source of disturbance, as budget deficits were modest in size.

The automatic co-ordination of monetary policy was brought about, first, through the willingness of each central bank to maintain a stable ratio of gold reserves to issues of currency and their readiness to increase the discount rate if the ratio was falling, to reduce it if the ratio was increasing. Thus, a deficit in the balance of payments, which led to an incipient gold outflow, was reversed by increases in the discount rate in the deficit country and a reduction in the surplus country. The short-run variability of interest rates and of currency in circulation was relatively high, especially in Germany, the United Kingdom, and the United States. The burden of adjustment of the balance of payments disequilibria was shared symmetrically between the United Kingdom and the other large industrial countries. As a result, actual international gold flows were relatively limited.

The second rule related to the determination of the world price level. As bank note circulation was linked to gold, the supply and demand of monetary gold proximately determined the world price level. In addition, the supply of monetary gold in the world was a declining function of the world price level. This was because the price of monetary gold was fixed—in pounds. With rising prices, the costs of extracting gold increased (barring technical progress in mining) and profits fell, and so gold production weakened. Inflationary pressures in the world economy as a whole therefore tended automatically to be countered in the long run by the mechanisms of the system.

The gold standard collapsed in 1914 when the internal convertibility of notes into gold was abolished. The war effort of individual countries led to high budget deficits, inflation, and a collapse in world trade. The gold standard which emerged after the First World War can hardly be called a system. Internal convertibility of bank notes into gold was not reintroduced in most countries. The world distribution of monetary gold was very uneven, with the United States possessing a very large fraction of it. The balance of payments adjustment mechanism therefore did not work smoothly, since domestic policy objectives were not subordinated to the external constraints. Moreover, free trade and free capital mobility were the exception rather than the rule. There was virtually no attempt at co-ordinating policies, nor an attempt by the United States to provide the necessary leadership. For example, budget deficits and external indebtedness were able to grow rapidly in Germany, especially in the second half of the 1920s.

The rise and fall of the Bretton Woods system also has lessons to offer [10]. The post-war era has had several sub-periods, each representing different mixes of the four strategic components of international economic systems: the trade regime, the exchange rate regime, the capital market regime, and the autonomous or co-operative management of macroeconomic policies. *The period as a whole supports the proposition that it is not possible to have free trade, freedom from capital restrictions, pegged exchange rates, and autonomous macroeconomic policies.* Such a system will not work because it allows inconsistent policies to develop.

The first post-war sub-period, lasting to the end of the 1950s, saw the return to free trade with a monetary order that pegged exchange rates to the dollar. However, countries were free to impose restrictions of capital movements, even encouraged to do so. This left considerable freedom in setting national economic policies, although the United States exerted a dominant influence.

In a second period, from the end of the 1950s, currencies started to become convertible again, the Eurocurrency market was born, and the system moved towards capital mobility. Problems of inconsistency began to emerge in the 1960s. Monetary co-operation was still of a high order and the consultative mechanisms of the OECD and IMF were effectively used. However, in the end it became evident that this 'soft' co-ordination was not enough to ensure consistency of the system, notably when the United States had recourse to inflationary financing of the Vietnam War.

A third period opened with the 1970s. Failure to reconcile national economic policies, coupled with high capital mobility between major financial centres, led to breakdown of the exchange rate system. The United States first suspended the gold convertibility of the dollar in 1971, and then the world switched to the floating exchange rate regime in 1973. The Eurocurrency market proved impossible to discipline. The sovereignty of national economic policies was to prevail.

As the years passed, it became increasingly clear that the elimination of the exchange rate constraint had restored only limited autonomy to macroeconomic policies, while the unrestricted floating of exchange rates risked undermining the open trade system and capital mobility. In this fourth period, the drawbacks of the new order (or 'non-system' as it is sometimes called) were recognized sooner in Europe than elsewhere, because the links between the European economies were particularly intense. The creation of the European Monetary System reintroduced the exchange rate constraint at a regional level in 1978, albeit with support from remaining capital controls in most participating countries, except Germany which became the centre of the system. At the international level, the United States began to reverse in 1985 its policy of neglect towards the exchange rate, but is unpreparedness so far to constrain its domestic policies to international needs still makes it difficult to envisage a structured system.

These examples support the proposition that economic proximity and interdependence create functional demands for monetary integration. They also warn that in the absence of strong rules or institutional foundations such endeavours tend to prove ephemeral, being incapable of withstanding the large disturbances that history continuously generates. This proved true again of the Snake of the early 1970s, and remains a warning for the European Monetary system, which failed to pass to its second (institutional) stage two years after its inception, as heads of state and government had originally agreed.

3. Economic and political communities. One of the main distinctions between the Community and most earlier integration episodes is that between political and economic contents of the integration process. Political motivation was essential in giving birth first to the Coal and Steel Community, then to the Treaty of Rome, and later to the demands of adhesion that led to three successive enlargements of the original Community of Six. The content of the Community, however, was economic. The consequence of this difference

between an economic and a political union can be seen both in the fact that in the EC the economic costs and benefits tend to be evaluated in rather narrow terms by Member States, and in the weakness of the central political structure. The Community does not have the political power to override grievances. In any case, current democratic usage is to resort rather readily to referenda both on issues of regional devolution as well as over membership of the Community or other fundamental steps (for example, in 1986 in Denmark over the Single European Act). The threat of secession, while happily not on the horizon in the Community at the present time, cannot be dismissed. *The cement of a political community is provided by indivisible public goods such as 'defence and security'. The cement of an economic community inevitably lies in the economic benefits it confers upon its members.*

PART C

APPRAISAL OF THE COMMUNITY SYSTEM TO DATE

5
Goods and Services Markets

5.1 Gains from trade and the opportunity costs of its stagnation

Recent economic analysis, both theoretical and empirical, supports the basic intuition behind the internal market programme, namely, that the opening of markets offers great welfare gains to the economy. (This leaves aside, for the moment, distribution questions). However, empirical evaluations of the gains from increased market integration are far from comprehensive, especially for the European Community. It is therefore appropriate that the Commission has recently commissioned an extensive programme of studies in this domain. These studies aim to cast more light on what has been called 'the costs of non-Europe'. The results will not be available until later this year. In the meantime, without wishing to prejudge the findings of these studies, it is possible to outline the nature of gains from increased trade and the results of a few empirical studies.

Gains from trade arise as goods and services are produced more efficiently and sold more competitively. This saves resources which can be used to produce additional goods and services. Real incomes rise as prices are reduced and as extra goods and services are produced. These gains, which are of course conditional upon the released resources being effectively re-employed, stem from three sources.

Longest established in economic literature is the notion of comparative advantage. Countries or regions endowed with different relative skills or natural resources gain by specializing in producing those goods or services for which they have the comparative advantage.

A different notion is that a wider market allows producers to achieve full advantage from economies of scale in production, R&D, and marketing. Specializations develop, leading to trade. Countries with similar endowments in skills and natural resources also find it beneficial to trade in this way. Much trade in the European Community is of this kind.

The question of economies of scale is linked to the third issue, that of concentration in the structure of industry and competition. With gains from increasing returns to scale come also dangers of fewer enterprises in a given branch, and oligopolistic or monopolistic market conditions. This in turn means less pressures for available efficiency gains to be achieved, and when they are achieved, risks of super-profits and difficulty of market entry on the part of those outside the oligopoly. Accordingly, an effective competition policy is crucial to the process of securing welfare gains from increased trade, and particularly so in relation to trade that exploits economies of scale rather than comparative advantage.

A fuller presentation of these concepts is given in the essay by Paul Krugman in Annex A, which also gives references to more detailed and technical sources.

In practice, trade within the European Community grew rapidly as a share of total intra- and extra-trade and as a share of GDP until about 1972. Since then, only the new Member States have seen major increases in intra-Community trade. For the original Member States, the stagnation of the share of intra-Community trade in GDP coincided with the slow-down in the macroeconomic growth rate. What can be said about the significance of the growth and then stagnation of intra-Community trade for the Community's general economic welfare?

The most detailed attempt to make a bridge between microeconomic studies of trends in trade and a macroeconomic assessment has been provided in a study by Owen [11]. Based on detailed studies of some major manufacturing industries such as cars, trucks, and household consumer durable goods, it estimated that increased trade generated gains in economic productivity equivalent to 50–100 per cent of the value of the additional trade. These figures may at first sight appear to be high, but are explained by the economic efficiency gains embodied in the entire production of sectors opened to effective competition, whether that production is exported or domestically sold. When trade becomes an important share of the total market, as is now the case within the Community for many manufactured goods sold to the private sector, production for the home market must respect conditions of external competition.

With the aid of further calculations scaling these findings in relation to the magnitude of total trade expansion, and the extent of induced pressures on the productivity growth also of service sectors, Owen's study concluded with a macroeconomic estimate of the total gains for the original six Member States of the Community. This was that the expansion of intra-Community trade since the inception of the EEC was associated with gains in productivity of the order of 3–6 per cent of total GDP.

Most of these gains took place in the years to 1973. Since then, among the original six Member States, there has been stagnation or even some decline in the share of intra-Community trade in the total of all trade. These trends have been documented in detail for individual countries and product categories [12,13]. Underlying the slight decline since 1973 in the average share of intra-EC imports in total EC imports for manufactured goods, the original EC Member States have seen a more pronounced reversal of their previously fast-growing intra-EC trade trends. The newer Member States have in recent years been converging on the original Member States in their trade structures, as intra-EC tariffs were eliminated. The United Kingdom's trade structure has been converging strongly on the pattern of the other large Member States. No doubt the new Mediterranean member countries will also follow this pattern. There is already evidence to this effect.

As regards the sectoral composition of these trends, the declining performance of intra-EC trade in relation to extra-EC imports is most sharp in the fields of mechanical and electrical engineering, electronic products, and transport equipment. These are typically branches with fast growth rates of demand in total world trade. By contrast, intra-EC trade has performed relatively more strongly (i.e. stagnated rather than declined) in intermediate products such as foodstuffs, textiles, leather, timber, paper, and non-metallic minerals and chemicals. These are in most cases product categories that are protected in the EC market either by the Common Agricultural Policy or by the high level of transport costs. Intermediate products are less subject within the Community to non-tariff barriers such as unharmonized technical standards and government procurement restrictions. By contrast, the potential for continuing trade growth appears to lie especially in branches which have a high R&D content and a high level of skilled labour in their value-added. It is these industries that suffer especially from non-tariff barriers.

Thus, while the initial trade-creating impact of the Community was associated with macroeconomically substantial gains, this impetus came to a halt in the course of the last decade, both at the level of market-opening measures and actual trade expansion. The new internal market programme, as set out in the Commission White Paper of 1985 [1], could represent a fresh impetus of macroeconomically significant proportions. The size of this possible impact cannot be asserted with any confidence. Some estimates [14,15] suggest that there could be a significant increase, over a period of years, in the growth rate of the industrialized countries as a result of a radical dismantling of trade barriers. While these estimates may be only very approximate, there is no doubt that the macroeconomic gains from increased trade in the Community, or opportunity costs of foregoing this, would be substantial.

5.2 Systemic issues in completing the goods and services markets

5.2.1 Tariffs and quotas

The European Community's first major achievement was to eliminate tariffs and quotas on intra-Community trade. However, in recent years, certain frontier tariffs and subsidies and quota restrictions on production have been reintroduced in sectors which were at the heart of the Community's foundation: agriculture and steel.

In agriculture, a system of border tariffs and subsidies, known as monetary compensatory amounts, was introduced in the 1970s to prevent exchange rate changes from immediately affecting the level of support prices expressed in national currency terms. These border adjustments were originally viewed as being (a) temporary, and (b) attributable to disorder in the exchange rate system. They are now thirteen years old, surviving the fact that the European Monetary System has largely re-established order in the exchange rate relations of the Community. In January 1987, the monetary compensatory amounts for the main products (beef, milk, cereals) were in the range of + 1.8 to + 2.9 per cent for Germany and the Netherlands, 0 for Belgium, − 1.1 to − 2.1 per cent for Italy, − 1.5 to − 8.0 per cent for France and − 18.4 to − 26.3 per cent for the United Kingdom. The pluses represent export subsidies or import taxes or the amounts by which national support prices are higher than the theoretical Community level in some countries; the minuses indicate the lower support prices. Average effective agricultural prices are on average about 4 per cent below their theoretical ECU level, with support prices in Germany and the Netherlands therefore about 6.5 per cent above the average.

The Community's subsidization of an above-average level of farm prices in Germany and the Netherlands is in contradiction with the laws of comparative advantage, as comparatively efficient agricultural producers in the rest of the Community are denied the possibility to increase market share. In a system which guarantees both purchase and price of unlimited quantities, the concept of comparative advantage is hardly relevant. However, with budgetary and production limitations now pressing hard upon the Common Agricultural Policy, the issue of how to allow for comparative advantage to prevail becomes relevant again.

Production quotas have been introduced for milk. Operated at the level of the individual farm, these quotas suppress competitive pressures and structural change within national economies, not just between them. The production quotas for milk have been announced as temporary measures for five years. However, the value of the quotas quickly become capitalized, which makes their removal increasingly difficult. As a second-best policy, it is argued that this quota system enables production to be cut more quickly and surely, thus helping ease the problem of dumping surpluses on world markets.

The system of production quotas in the steel sector was established in 1980 under the temporary 'manifest crisis' conditions that were recognized at that time. By 1986, some small steps were decided for phasing out the production quotas, with certain products amounting to about 20 per cent of all steel production being liberalized. The Community and Member States have also been programming together capacity reductions and the phasing out of state subsidies. However, in the meantime, steel users are faced with non-competitive input prices, steel producers proceed with their 'rationalizations' without having to face fully competitive conditions either internally or externally.

Other internal quota systems are also sanctioned by Community policies. Under the multi-fibre agreement of the GATT, the Community has negotiated a matrix of bilateral quotas for individual textile products, specified by each Member State of the EC and forty-five textile-exporting developing countries. The Common Fisheries Policy determines tonnages of total allowable catches for the fleet of each Member State, but this is more defendable on conservation grounds. There is also between countries a system of bilateral road haulage quota (permits) which is, however, being liberalized gradually (see further below).

Elimination of these restraints on competition in agriculture, steel, fisheries, and textiles hardly feature in the White Paper [1], but are of much greater economic importance than many of the smaller new initiatives proposed. These sectors account for about 6 per cent of total GDP in the Community as a whole. Quotas on production or trade are an extreme form of protection or market rigidity and deny the possibility for the Common Market to deliver its potential benefits. *These quota regimes have tended to emerge in sectors suffering from crises of excess capacity. Some of these industries or agricultural branches are fields in which the new Member States might expect to increase their market shares on grounds of comparative advantage, and the Community should indeed assure these countries fair opportunities for expansion as their economies are subjected to the full impact of Community competition. The only proper solution to this problem is to avoid creating new quota systems in the organization of Community markets, and to phase out existing systems in a fair way.*

5.2.2 Competition policy and subsidies

The White Paper [1] is also only brief on this subject, doubtless because Community powers here are already substantial.

The increase in subsidies to industry, while difficult to assess in monetary terms for statistical reasons, is evident in the number of cases notified by Member States to the Commission. Until the early 1970s, the annual number of notified cases was 20 to 30, this covering both aid regimes and individual cases. In 1977, the number passed 100, and in recent years has risen to between 150 and 200. The Commission has in recent years taken negative decisions on about 20 cases per year, whereas in earlier years the normal number was 1 to 3. However, the amount of industrial subsidies appears now to be beginning to decline again as budgetary constraints have tightened and the philosophy of public policy has become more critical.

The Commission's policy, following the Treaty, has been to object to state aids which distort competition, but not to other aid regimes. This is in line with the principle that the Community should be concerned where there are important effects on external trading conditions. In practice, Community policy towards state aids has been mainly concentrated on regional aids, subsidy regimes specific to certain sectors of industry, employment subsidies, and R&D subsidies.

Regional aids in particular are viewed relatively favourably, subject to a Community regulation of the zoning of regions within each Member State, and respect of maximum rates of grant equivalent for zones with different degrees of regional handicap.

As regards sector-specific aid regimes, the cases of coal, steel, cars, ship-building, and textiles have been the most important. The general criteria used by the Commission to evaluate such aids include whether capacity reduction is planned, whether the amounts of aid are limited in time and degressive, whether the firms participate in the financing of investment, and whether the firm is likely to regain financial viability in due course. The regime for coal subsidies is less stringent than some others, and this is justifiable since production is declining in all countries and there is no problem of Community excess capacity. Aids to the textile and steel sectors have now been largely phased out, after a long adjustment period. Recent Community agreements limit aids to ship-building to 28 per cent of the value of sales.

In 1985, the Commission adopted a new approach towards R&D expenditures, which in general terms was more positive towards state aids of this type because of their strategic importance in industrial policy. A high ceiling of 50 per cent was established for the maximum amount of public aids contributing to the research programmes of private enterprises. Also, competition policy towards private enterprises has become more favourably disposed to collaborative R&D projects of Community interest.

Aid regimes for small and medium-sized enterprises are on the whole favourably viewed by the Commission, since they imply relatively small effects on external trading conditions. Employment aids for training and youth employment are also viewed favourably, but employment subsidy regimes which are firm- or sector-specific are viewed critically.

Commission policy towards subsidies appears in general to be managed in conformity with the most relevant principle, that is the effective importance for trading conditions between countries. Where these effects are weak, national governments must be the arbiter of wise versus unwise subsidy policies. However, there are two policy issues to which further attention is given later: (a) how the general thrust of Community competition policy should be affected by the internal market programme, and (b) how to respond to a manifest practical problem faced by the Commission with its limited staff in handling the enormous number of aid schemes that exist.

5.2.3 Government procurement restrictions

Government procurement is estimated to amount to nearly 200 billion ECUs per year in the Community, or about 6 per cent of GDP. This figure is probably an underestimate, since it does not cover all state enterprises. It includes defence procurement, which amounts to about a quarter of the total.

There can be no doubt that government procurement is to a large extent done on terms that are internationally weakly competitive. The import content of government procurement tends to be in the range of 10 to 20 per cent on average for the larger EC Member States, according to the type of product. For the whole economy (i.e. private and public purchases), the import content for the same product categories averages 15 to 50 per cent. By contrast, in small, very open economies, such as Denmark, the import content of government procurement is much more similar to the economy-wide average. Studies of price differences between countries of the Community for products bought by government suggest that economies of the order of 25 per cent are often foregone in not buying at the lowest costs offered on competitive markets. These various indicators suggest that economies of the order of 1 to 2 per cent of GDP could be obtained through competitive government purchasing in the Community.

Competitive tendering is required by Community directives for public purchasing in general terms, but important sectors are excluded (energy-generating and transport equipment, telecommunications, water supply equipment). In addition, the effectiveness of existing directives, even for the included sectors, is weak, with most contracts not published in the ways required and negotiated without open competition. To counter these problems, legislation was passed in December 1986 to ensure more transparency in tendering procedures. Commission proposals are being prepared for extending the coverage of Community directives to the excluded sectors.

Under the Single European Act, the passing of legislation in this field comes under the qualified majority voting rule. In addition, the Community's Treaty powers in the area of competition policy (Art. 90) allow the Commission some scope to take action against uncompetitive practices irrespective of the extent of such directives.

Some advances are being made currently in the opening of procurement for the difficult but important field of telecommunications equipment. The policy approach here is a complex and progressive one: concentration on new products, introduction of minimum quotas for open procurement, links to technical standardization, the combination of Community finance and open procurement rules for some large cross-frontier projects. This example suggests that in sectors of strategic importance more is required to open markets than a simple legalistic approach.

The scene is therefore set for the Community to make significant progress in opening up competition in the public procurement area. This could also subsequently put the Community in a more favourable position to negotiate in the GATT improvements to the weakly effective international code in this field. The restructuring of several industries, like energy-generating equipment, railway equipment, and office machinery, could be quite drastic as a result. This also has implications for strategic industrial policies and policy towards state enterprises and privatization, which is discussed more directly later.

5.2.4 Technical standards

Community policy and decision-making methods towards the removal of technical barriers to trade have been undergoing major reform since 1984. The Community's traditional approach was based on harmonization directives which had to be agreed by unanimity. By the end of 1983, 158 directives had been adopted by the Council. But this was slow progress, with new national technical regulations accumulating at a much faster pace. For example, in the field of voluntary technical standards, the German DIN institute had by 1983 produced a total of 23,000 standards, and equivalent organizations in France and the United Kingdom have together accumulated as many again [16].

In the early 1980s, it was evident that a new approach was called for [17]. The White Paper [1] confirms and reinforces a set of principles that emerged in 1984 and 1985. Three of the most important were: (*a*) concentration of the Community's actions on satisfying objectives for the health and safety of citizens, rather than on comprehensive regulatory requirements, (*b*) wide application of the principle of mutual recognition of national tests and certification, and (*c*) a strengthened capacity to produce European standards where appropriate, partly through endowing relevant technical organizations—such as CEN (Comité Européen de Normalisation) and CENELEC (Comité Européen de Normalisation Électronique)—with powers to draw up European standards on a qualified majority voting basis. The Single European Act further strengthens the capacity of the Community to act in this area, since future directives for technical standards can now be adopted by the Council by qualified majority vote.

At the present time, the new mutual recognition approach is being tried out on a number of test cases. The length of technical texts for adoption by the legislature is reduced drastically, which is highly desirable. Also to be welcomed is the increasing emphasis placed upon the setting of standards for new products, such as telecommunications and microelectronics. The capacity of European public and private sectors to establish critical norms early in the product development cycle is an important aspect of the Community's strategy for industrial competitiveness world-wide.

5.2.5 *Transport services*

Until recently, almost no action had been taken by the Council to free road, sea, or air transport from a mass of restrictions on market entry and effective competition. This even led in 1985 to an action brought in the European Court of Justice, which found that the Council had neglected its duties in this area. Recently, some liberalizing action has been taken. In 1986, it was decided to raise the number of permits for road haulage in the Community by 40 per cent per year until 1992, to the point that competition in international trucking would increasingly become effective. In 1986, the Council agreed measures to open up competition in maritime shipping between countries, but left coastal shipping services within Member States unliberalized.

The Community has long been concerned by the subsidization of railways, but has had little success with efforts to control this field. It may be doubted whether the Community should attempt to do so. The motivation of these subsidies comes from a mix of social and regional policy objectives which are not strongly relevant to the Community, and their economic impact is quite diffuse.

Civil aviation is now easily the most important target of Community transport policy. It has still seen only little progress in the introduction of competition, in spite of a considerable build-up of negotiations in the Council and warnings of legal actions that the Commission may bring against governments and airlines. Scheduled air transport in Europe has been restricted by a very comprehensive array of barriers to competition: prices, revenues, capacity, and market entry have all been fixed in a web of bilateral agreements between governments maintained under the 1944 Chicago Convention. This system has only been departed from in the Community under the highly circumscribed 1984 Directive for scheduled interregional air services. As a result, prices must be substantially higher and service substantially poorer than would obtain in a competitive market. Comparison between the densest routes in Europe with similar routes in the United States show higher prices in Europe of the order of 40 to 75 per cent. Moreover, in Europe 50 to 60 per cent of passengers pay the full price, whereas in the United States, only 15 per cent do so. The economic and social problems of restructuring the civil aviation business are not particularly difficult in comparison with many other branches of the economy. Employment issues are relatively slight, in the sense that service networks will have to remain in all countries and regions. Major resources, such as aircraft and skilled personnel, can move between enterprises more easily than in many industries.

The Single Europe Act means more scope for majority voting in the transport field. The jurisdiction of the Community in the field of civil aviation has been clarified and extended by recent Court of Justice decisions (*Nouvelles Frontières*, etc.). The slow progress in the Council over liberalizing civil aviation has led some countries (the United Kingdom, the Netherlands, Belgium, Germany, and Ireland) to make bilateral agreements, freeing market entry and prices on certain routes. These agreements have some potential for putting pressure upon other governments whose airlines may lose market share as a result. This is an example of the possibility to introduce competition among rules of public policy (this is discussed as a general principle later).

The freeing of transport services for open competition is of critical importance for the whole of the Community to facilitate commercial integration and also to advance the 'people's Europe'. It is particularly in the interests of peripheral regions and countries as a means to overcome locational disadvantages. These market-liberalizing measures are therefore particularly favourable to the cohesion of the Community.

5.2.6 Financial services

Insurance, banking, and the marketing of securities add up to a sector of the economy that accounts for around 7 per cent of GDP, a share which is growing strongly. The economic importance of the financial services sector is even greater when account is taken of the size of capital flows that it mediates, the risk of instability that is inherent in financial markets, and the links between finance and all the other fields of economic activity.

The liberalization across the Community of the financial services industry is conditioned by three special factors. First, the supply of these services is deeply tied in with the ability to move capital freely from one country to another. Secondly, the world market dimension to financial markets is a dominating factor. Thirdly, technological change is currently causing a profound restructuring of the industry. Indeed, the three main branches—insurance, banking, and securities markets—are tending to become more closely integrated where liberalization has gone farthest.

These factors have profound implications for the design of policies of regulation and supervision of these services. The opening of capital markets and technological advances in the world-wide electronic transfer of funds means that all countries have to be more concerned with the soundness of the international system. On the other hand, the rapidity of technical and structural changes within the industry means that supervisory authorities have to be able to react very flexibly to new situations.

The strategy for financial services proposed by the Commission basically consists of two elements. First, the harmonization of essential requirements on prudential controls and the protection of the investor, depositor, and consumer; second, freedom to provide services of the whole Community by any company established in a member country on the basis of the principle of mutual recognition and 'home country control', meaning that foreign financial products or institutions should be monitored by the supervisory authorities of the country of the parent company.

As regards *insurance*, the right of establishment in other member countries has been secured. However, except in the case of co-insurance, there has been little progress on freedom to supply services across frontiers, and national markets therefore remain largely segmented. Insurance companies in one country cannot directly contract in another country. Partly as a result of this, premiums for insurances covering virtually homogeneous risks, like fire insurance policies, vary widely from country to country. Important test cases were taken by the Court of Justice in this area in December 1986. Basically, the Court refused to endorse the full opening of the insurance market in the absence of further legislation by the Council that would harmonize essential regulations concerning prudential standards. By contrast, in the area of co-insurance, the Court judged that the existing directive was sufficient to justify open competition on the basis of the 'home country principle'.

The integration of *banking* is more advanced than is the case with insurance. The right of establishment, as in the case of insurance, has been secured, but its full exercise is still subject to restrictions. Where capital movements have been liberalized, there is generally freedom to supply banking services.

Nevertheless, the market is still far from fully integrated. The definition of activities permitted to banks varies widely from country to country, and so do regulations regarding solvency and liquidity ratios, reserve requirements, concentration of risks, and so forth. In preparing proposals for Community legislation in these areas, account has to be taken of steps towards international harmonization world-wide.

Within the Community, banks of one Member State wanting to conduct business in another may still face restrictions on the ability to establish a subsidiary, or the number of branches of a foreign bank and their location may be circumscribed. There are unnecessary entry-cost barriers to setting up branches in most member countries. Foreign banks may also suffer from discrimination impeding them from competing on an equal footing for the management of local issues of securities.

Progress in legislating the minimum harmonization requirements in these services will lead next to the question of how the regulatory and executive powers should be organized in an integrated market. According to one traditional model, the Commission would be responsible for the implementing regulations of Member States, while the Member States would be responsible for the executive responsibilities. Such a complete separation would probably harm the smooth functioning of the single financial services market. It therefore may be advisable to make an exception to normal Community institutional rules and entrust a mixture of regulatory and executive powers to technical bodies (like the EC Banking Advisory Committee) which group together national experts and the Commission.

In general, the opening of the internal market for financial services will have very far-reaching implications for the regulatory and supervisory authorities. The Community will no doubt have to be prepared for considerable innovations in its models of harmonization, mutual recognition, and co-ordinated supervision in order to handle the dimensions of the task—namely, the combination of very rapid technical change, prudential risks of a high order, and strong links to monetary policy.

5.2.7 Indirect tax harmonization and fiscal frontiers

Introduction of the value-added tax (VAT) and elimination of a host of earlier sales taxes has been the Community's major achievement in the tax harmonization field. The value-added tax has the important quality of neutrality with respect to resource allocation, especially in comparison with the taxes it replaced, which often had uncertain and arbitrary incidences (e.g. the cumulative turnover tax) or were used for purposes of trade protection.

The 'White Paper' [1] now seeks an approximation of value-added and excise tax rates with a view to suppressing fiscal obstacles at intra-EC frontiers. Details of these proposals are expected to be published soon by the Commission.

For VAT, the 'White Paper' outlined two proposals, intended respectively as interim and final solutions to this problem. The interim solution would be for value-added tax assessment to be made 'inland' rather than at the frontier for enterprises which make value-added tax returns. This is the proposal of the so-called 14th VAT Directive. It is already the method used in the Benelux. According to this system, the VAT payment due at the time of import is delayed until the importer makes his general VAT declaration.

For the definitive regime, the White Paper proposes both a negotiated approximation of VAT rates within bands, and a change in the principles of VAT collection. Importers would buy goods inclusive of the VAT of the supplying country, rather than VAT-free as at present. However, a clearing mechanism between fiscal administrations would return to the importing country the VAT revenues paid to the exporter.

In the absence of detailed proposals and supporting analysis, the Group has not attempted to evaluate the strategy outlined by the Commission. There are important empirical issues to be clarified, for example the relative administrative costs of the different proposals for VAT, and the extent to which indirect tax differences can be accommodated with the effective suppression of frontier controls without excessive trade distortions. Where VAT differences can be offset by other differences in tax burdens, labour costs, or exchange rate adjustments, it is not particularly important that VAT rates be harmonized from the point of view of production costs. This is separate, however, from the question of how much cross-frontier shopping might follow from the suppression of fiscal frontiers, taking into account voluntary adjustments of tax rates that countries suffering revenue losses might make.

It may be noted that the United States has open state frontiers despite wide differences in some excise duties such as tobacco. Sales taxes there range from zero to 7.5 per cent and are not levied on out-of-state sales. Theoretically, these inter-state fiscal frontiers are not abolished, and the Community's approach to what constitutes abolition of fiscal frontiers should similarly be reasonably pragmatic.

The objective of suppressing fiscal frontier controls should be supported, and given effect in ways that minimize the burden of indirect tax harmonization. Fiscal harmonization is one of the few areas of internal market legislation in the Community that still requires unanimity.

6
Labour Markets

6.1 Labour migration issues

Drafted at a time of nearly full employment, the Treaty of Rome viewed labour markets essentially in the context of the Common Market, and thus laid down the right of Community nationals to work or to be self-employed in any Member State. The Treaty was also concerned with the extra retraining of labour required by the structural change associated with increased trade, hence creation of the Social Fund.

There are several economic arguments which point to benefits from the mobility of labour. Where the marginal productivity of labour is different as between regions, migration will increase the income of the individual and of the aggregate economy. Migrants' remittances to his home region may also mean that all regional economies benefit, although this is not necessarily always the case. The mobility of labour can also help the economy to adapt to structural changes, especially where exchange rates are fixed or nearly so. These arguments are usually related to the case of substantial net flows of migrants from depressed regions to buoyant regions.

A different pattern of migration, and one which may be increasingly pertinent for the European Community, is one in which there are fluid exchanges of individuals with particular skills in all directions, without particularly significant net flows of mass migration. This second pattern is analogous to the distinction made in trade theory between inter-industry and intra-industry trade. The latter category confers benefits through increasing competition and specialization at fine levels of economic detail.

These general economic arguments are relevant to how the figures on migratory movements are to be interpreted, and how the Community's policies towards labour movements should be viewed.

Direct barriers to the migration of workers and the self-employed have been effectively eliminated among the first nine Member States. For the three newest Member States, the same rights will be fully applicable from 1988 for Greece, and from 1993 for Spain and Portugal. Until these dates, work permits may still be required before employment offers can be accepted.

The Community has also gone far in establishing rules for the co-ordination of national social security systems to prevent migrant workers from within the Community suffering discrimination or loss of cumulative benefits. This co-ordination system covers all the major branches of social security (sickness, old-age pensions, unemployment benefits, etc.).

Recent policy initiatives have sought to enlarge the list of protected professions for which the mutual recognition of qualifications is accepted between Member States. Doctors, dentists, vets, midwives, architects, and so on are now mutually recognized, and the self-employed have rights of establishment. Further proposals are being discussed. To minimize the burden of harmonization, the principle of maximum mutual recognition deserves full support in this field.

Much remains to be done in some major grey areas, where formal barriers may be less important. The mutual acceptability of vocational training qualifications, the mobility of students, and the openness of university appointments are all areas to which the White Paper [1] draws attention, and where new initiatives are envisaged.

These actions to open up the professions and exchanges in higher education are very much what is needed to facilitate migratory movements of the intra-industry category, rather than that of the mass migration category. The former category is surely in line with needs of the modern economy, and much less problematic politically than mass migration. Many scientific and academic professions in Europe explain their relative weakness compared with the United States in terms of the small size of segmented national markets in Europe. The economic losses for Europe occur not only through the relative weakness of specialization and competition, but also through substantial 'brain-drain' emigration to the United States of Europeans who do attain professional eminence at the world level.

While statistics on migratory movements are not very good, it is clear that mass migration within Europe has stopped in the last decade. Greece, Spain, and Portugal have all ceased to be countries of net emigration, although it is possible that when the transitional restrictions are removed in 1988 and 1993 renewed migratory flows may occur. Within the original Member States, Italy has during the past decade become a country of remigration home. Immigration from outside the Community is now severely restricted, except that for Turkey special arrangements exist by virtue of the association agreement between the Community and this country.

The fact that mass migration has stopped does not at all mean that the freedom of movement of labour within the Community is no longer an important matter. On the contrary, it is increasingly important to assure truly competitive labour market conditions at the microeconomic level of individual professions and skills, since this complements the particular structure of intra-industry trade flows that is predominant within the Community.

6.2 Wider labour market issues

The Community institutions are concerned with a wide range of labour market issues, but it is controversial how extensive these responsibilities should be.

In the social policy field, there has been some Community legislation on health and safety regulations, and some also on employment regulations (equal pay, conditions of collective dismissal). Further regulations have been proposed by the Commission but not accepted yet by the Council (e.g. on conditions of part-time and temporary work, and parental leave). As regards social security regimes, there has been no attempt to harmonize with Community directives, but this is sometimes advocated in political debate, for example through the setting of minimum standards of benefits.

As regards labour market measures such as vocational training and job creation initiatives, the Social Fund is active in funding, usually at a rate of 50 per cent, schemes that meet criteria negotiated at the Community level. The resources of the Social Fund are quite small in relation to national actions of the same kinds. The Social Fund's original purpose of supporting the retraining of workers because of the opening of markets has become increasingly hard to separate from the vaster problem of mass unemployment. (These issues are further addressed below in the context of reform of the structural funds.)

The case for and against Community intervention in these various aspects of labour and social policies may be guided by two principles: (*a*) the importance of cross-frontier spill-over effects, i.e. whether the policies in question have sharp external effects, or are primarily of domestic concern; and (*b*) the priority need to find solutions to the problem of unemployment.

As regards health and safety regulations, the Community has a reason to be involved where these have a sharp influence over the location of investments. The production of dangerous products or processes, such as certain chemicals or nuclear materials, should clearly not be allowed to concentrate in countries that might be prepared to adopt lax standards. In this kind of case, cross-frontier effects may be important, so Community regulations would be warranted. Otherwise, maximum recourse to mutual recognition of standards, as advocated in the White Paper [1], is recommendable.

Social security systems and employment protection laws are highly relevant to the employment question. They contribute significantly to labour costs, either directly or indirectly. They affect in important ways the reaction of the labour market to the unemployment problem. On the other hand, policy adjustments in these areas generate relatively weak external, cross-frontier impacts. These are arguments favouring a decentralized (national level) approach to policy in these fields. Countries should be free to experiment with policy adjustment in the search of more efficient means of achieving the double objectives of a high level of employment and high standards of social security. Harmonization of policies would not seem to be recommendable, especially where the initial situation is one of massive labour market disequilibrium. Where policies are seen to be successful, convergence is to be expected. The processes of social dialogue at the Community level between employers, trade unions, and government can help this convergence materialize.

The principle of subsidiarity recommends minimal responsibility on the part of the Community for many aspects of social policy, but the question of convergence of labour costs is vital in the context of increasing monetary integration. We return to this later.

7
Capital markets

Open and competitive capital markets are an integral part of an efficient process of allocation of resources. Enterprises need to be able to decide upon their investment and commercial strategies without the constraints of segmented, and therefore locally limited, capital markets. Savers need to be able to choose their most profitable investment strategies across the entire economy. Only an open capital market can provide adequate information to enable an efficient allocation of resources to take place in a given economic region. These are the reasons why the abolition of obstacles to the free movement of capital is stated by the Treaty of Rome as one of the fundamental components of the Common Market.

The implementation of this part of the Treaty made rapid progress with two directives approved in 1960 and 1962, but stood still or regressed thereafter. In the late 1970s, only Germany had a completely open capital market, while extensive restrictions were operating in France, Italy, the United Kingdom, Denmark, and Ireland. Safeguard clauses provided for by the Treaty of Rome (Art. 108) were widely used, to effectively re-establish several of the obstacles that had been removed by the 1960 and 1962 directives and this was tolerated by the Commission.

Meanwhile, starting in the late 1950s, the Euromarket, based initially in London and Luxemburg as an 'off-shore' dollar capital market to evade certain regulations in the United States, grew very large, became diversified in its currency denomination, and in many ways performed the function of an integrated international market. By 1985, the size of the international money market in EC national currencies and European Currency Units (ECUs) was over 260 billion ECUs. The Euro-Deutschmark money market amounted to around 35 per cent of the German M3 money stock. The relative size of the off-shore market was, however, still minor for other currencies like the French franc or the Italian lira, with respective magnitudes of 3 per cent and 0.5 per cent. The international bond market in European currencies in 1985 saw over 320 billion ECUs of bond issues, compared with 335 billion ECUs of domestic bond issues in Member States (exclusive of Belgium and Luxemburg).

A survey conducted by the Bank of England in March 1986 estimated that turnover in the London foreign exchange market averaged $90 billion a day, compared with $50 billion in New York and $48 billion in Tokyo. Out of the $90 billion turnover, only 9 per cent was accounted for by transactions carried out directly with non-bank customers (although it should be noted that a single transaction with a commercial customer may give rise to a number of other foreign exchange deals in the currency market). These daily turnover figures are enormous compared to the daily average of the value of world exports and imports of goods and services in 1985, which equalled some $15.5 billion.

Since the mid-1979 dismantlement of exchange controls in the United Kingdom, a new trend of liberalization was set that gradually spread over the whole Community. The openness of national markets, however, is still uneven between Member States. Germany, the Netherlands and the United Kingdom are completely open. Belgium and Denmark are very largely, though incompletely, open. In France, important measures of liberalization were decided in 1986. The other Member States retain an important array of controls, but are gradually removing existing restrictions.

For the four largest EC economies, gross capital flows (average of in- and outflows) in 1984 ranged between 15 billion ECUs in the case of Italy to 50 billion ECUs in the case of the United Kingdom, amounting to 3 per cent and 8 per cent of the respective GDPs. Net capital flows are relatively small in relation to the gross flows (typically ranging from zero up to half the size of the gross flows). This fact, however, does not mean that their economic significance is correspondingly slight. As in the case of migration of labour, the two-way flow of production factors across frontiers is largely part of the process of competition and specialization at the microeconomic level. Thus, analogues to the distinction between inter-industry and intra-industry trade are found in all three branches of the common market: trade, labour and capital. Also, interest rates on domestic markets have shown a tendency to converge and to move together, a further indication that financial integration is progressing within Europe.

The process of creating a single European capital market was delayed by the difficulty of reconciling it with an exchange rate constraint (first determined by the Bretton Woods system, and later by the EMS), with non-convergent macroeconomic developments, and a desired degree of national autonomy in the conduct of monetary policy. In 1983, a Commission communication on financial integration reopened the debate on these issues at the Community level. Capital liberalization was taken up actively in this White Paper [1].

The Community's actions in this area fall under four headings:

1. Directives to remove obstacles on capital movements.
2. Regulatory requirements to ensure the stability and efficient functioning of capital markets.
3. Tax harmonization measures to remove fiscal distortions.
4. Borrowing and lending activity conducted directly by the Community institutions.

To remove obstacles to the freedom of *capital movements*, a directive was passed by the Council in late 1986 enlarging the categories of capital transactions that are subject to the unconditional obligation of liberalization (adding share capital, and bond issues, and long-term trade credits to the prior list). The Commission has undertaken to formulate in the first half of 1987 a further proposal on how to proceed to total dismantling of exchange controls. This ultimate step would have major implications for the economic and monetary system of the Community. We return to these issues later (section 12.1).

As regards *regulatory requirements*, some useful steps have been taken at the Community level to harmonize company accounting and auditing standards. For example, Member States are currently implementing a 1983 directive requiring the publication of consolidated accounts, which is a basic information requirement not earlier satisfied in several Member States. The 1980 directive on the co-ordination of prospectus requirements for the listing of shares on stock exchanges does not provide for the total harmonization of listing conditions. A Commission proposal for the harmonization of public offer prospectus requirements for various sorts of securities is in an advanced stage of negotiation in the Council. This proposed directive draws once more on the mutual recognition principle. This and other recent Commission proposals in this area would facilitate further the access of firms to the capital market of other Member States. Further Commission proposals on 'insider dealing' and the freedom to supply investment services are expected later in 1987.

As regards *tax harmonization*, the Commission made proposals on corporation tax systems as long ago as 1975, but no agreement has been reached in the Council. However, corporate taxation and the related issue of capital taxation are of the greatest importance, as they may shape the financial system and may divert capital flows from the most efficient uses. In the course of 1987 the Commission will set out its current thinking on how to progress on company taxation. Our own views on the reform of corporation taxes on a harmonized basis are set out in 11.3 and Annex B.

The Community's own *borrowing and lending* activities have grown rapidly, from a small base, in recent years. The total of such operations never exceeded 1 billion ECUs per year before 1974, but rose to the 8 billion ECU level by 1985. Impetus for this expansion came from the operations of the European Investment Bank and the New Community Instrument (a borrowing power of the Commission) in the less prosperous regions of the Community, and from loans for energy, infrastructure and small and medium-sized enterprises. The Community institutions borrow on the most favourable terms in international capital markets and on-lend in countries whose enterprises or public authorities could have difficulties in attracting this capital on comparable terms, thus deliberately reaching over the barriers represented by national capital market controls and limited local capital markets. The management of Community borrowing and lending activities has so far succeeded in combining the function of effectively promoting investment with the requirement of following orthodox banking criteria. The Community institutions have also taken a leading role in the marketing of ECU-denominated financial assets on international capital markets, an aspect of capital market integration that links to the development of the European Monetary System.

The integration of the Community's capital market is a multi-faceted task, involving the liberalization of capital movements, the harmonization of certain regulatory requirements, tax harmonization issues, and direct borrowing and lending operations by the Community institutions. A considerable momentum of efforts to progress along these general lines has now been established, but much remains to be done.

8
Macroeconomic Policy

8.1 European Monetary System

The Community's first attempt at monetary integration did not survive in a stormy international economic environment. Following the adoption of the objective of economic and monetary union at the Community summit of March 1972, a Community exchange rate system was inaugurated in April of that year. This was the so-called 'snake in the tunnel', whereby Community currencies were to respect 2.25 per cent fluctuation margins amongst themselves, within a set of wider parities related to the dollar. When the dollar floated in 1973, the Snake was left to function on its own. Shortly later, the pound, the lira and the French franc left the Snake, with the French franc subsequently entering and leaving again. Economic policy strategies in the wake of the first oil shock were very divergent, and the shrinking of the Snake to a grouping of a few currencies of small countries around the Deutschmark reflected this.

The Community's second attempt, the European Monetary System (EMS), has been far more successful. It adopted the 2.25 per cent fluctuation margins from the Snake, with Italy, however, joining with wider (6 per cent) margins. The European Currency Unit (ECU) was given a central place in the system, for example in relation to the mechanisms for parities, reserves, credit, and the 'divergence indicator'. All the then Member States joined fully except the United Kingdom, which has remained on the outside edge of the system (the pound is in the ECU and the Bank of England participates in the ECU-creating mechanism, but the pound is not in the exchange rate mechanism). The EMS has proved to be a stable system notwithstanding the fact that shocks from the oil market and dollar exchange rate movements, comparable to those of the early 1970s, have been hitting the system repeatedly since it was set up in 1978. Some commentators have suggested that the EMS survived the second oil shock only because it coincided with a period of dollar strength and Deutschmark weakness, which helped the other EMS currencies to maintain their value relative to the Deutschmark. However, over the last two years, the dollar has lost much of its earlier gains, and the EMS has experienced only a moderate increase in the amplitude and frequency of realignments of parities.

The success of the EMS in relation to its objective of establishing a zone of monetary stability in Europe can be inferred from indicators measuring the variability of nominal exchange rates and the convergence price and cost trends among participating countries. Nominal exchange rate variability has been reduced. The average rate of consumer price rise in the EMS group of countries has declined steadily from over 11 per cent in 1980 to 2.5 per cent in 1986, compared to 3.5 per cent in the 1960s. Nominal wage costs and unit labour costs have converged even more than in the 1960s.

A traditional case for exchange rate stabilization has been based on the reduced uncertainty offered to traders and investors, and hence the increased willingness to invest in production and marketing systems aimed at the whole of the market. To these microeconomic arguments must be added issues of macroeconomic stabilization strategy. Adhesion to the EMS has given the monetary authorities of formerly weak currencies an anchor for price stability. Commitment to the EMS has given to these currencies some of the monetary stability features of the leading currency of the system, the Deutschmark. Since the disinflation process is only a gradual one, the countries with low inflation at the outset obtain a certain advantage in terms of competitivity. On the other hand, for the countries seeking to reduce inflation, pegging of the exchange rate on a strong currency can help lower the interest rate required for a given stabilization strategy, thus lessening the macroeconomic adjustment costs of such a strategy. Also, the clarity of exhange rate commitments within the EMS has often given a valuable point of reference for the co-ordination of other elements of policy, notably as regards budgetary policy and labour cost trends. This was clearly seen in important policy adjustments in Belgium and Denmark in 1982, and France in 1983. Overall, the stability of the EMS, compared with the Snake, points to the central importance of having convergent domestic policies towards the reduction of inflation.

These comparative successes of the EMS should not lead to excessive satisfaction with the status quo. The evolution of the EMS has been disappointing so far in relation to its founders' intentions to move to a second stage that would include stronger institutional developments. In 1982, there was extensive work in the relevant Community bodies in preparing possible institutional advances [18]. No agreement could be reached on this, and subsequent attempts to prepare packages of measures to strengthen the EMS have given only marginal results. The role of the ECU has advanced only in private markets, where a full range of money and capital market instruments have developed over the last four years. The EMS has led to very little strengthening of the Community's presence in international monetary affairs. The ECU has not emerged as the operational pivot of exchange rate relations between the United States, Japan, and Europe.

The institutional fragility of the EMS will be tested in fundamental ways by the process of removing exchange controls, as envisaged in the White Paper [1]. The degree of convergence of inflation rates and co-ordination of monetary policies will have to be raised to a very high standard if the present exchange rate system is not to be destabilized. These issues are therefore taken up more thoroughly later in this report.

8.2 The wider system of economic policy co-ordination

The case for economic policy co-ordination rests upon the need to correct for biases in national policy-making that tend to arise where the impact of policy adjustments tends to leak out across national frontiers to an important degree. For example, in a small, open economy, budgetary actions intended to stimulate demand will see a significant part of the increased spending flow abroad, with costs to the balance of payments and less benefits for domestic activity. In such a situation, individual countries may take an unduly pessimistic view of the efficiency of budgetary policy adjustments. In the event of a co-ordinated stimulative action, these leakages of benefits would be partly offset, with each country importing as well as exporting benefits.

Analogous phenomena exist on the side of monetary policy. A country wishing to reduce its inflation rate as a first priority, and which tightens its monetary policy in an uncoordinated policy setting (i.e. with a floating rather than managed exchange rate), will achieve extra price stabilization benefits as a result of an appreciation of its exchange rate. However, the countries experiencing depreciating exchange rates will, as a result, be importing a price-rising effect. Thus, unco-ordinated monetary policy may lead to a competitive process of monetary policy restrictions, leading to a more depressed international economy than policy-makers had intended.

The Community's most systematic attempt to assure the co-ordination of budgetary policy is seen in the Council's decision of 1974 aimed at the convergence of economic policies in the Community, known as the '1974 Convergence Decision' [19]. According to this text, the Commission and the Council should work together to establish Community guidelines for the main aggregates of budgetary policy (budget deficit, expenditures, revenues) in quantified form. The Commission proposes a Community view of desirable national budget aggregates. The Council is required to adopt these guidelines, and bring them to the attention of national parliaments so that they can be taken into account in legislative processes. Mid-year reviews are provided for to examine whether these guidelines need to be maintained or revised. The guidelines, together with supporting analysis, are published in an Annual Economic Report.

In the course of over a decade's experience, the system envisaged under the Convergence Decision has revealed two fundamental weaknesses. One is quasi-constitutional, the second relates to the philosophy of economic policy.

The constitutional issue is how the Community institutions and national authorities are supposed to share responsibility for the policy-making process. The authors of the Convergence Decision would have the Council deciding on policy guidelines, with a view to these being taken into account by national authorities. However, the Council is composed of the same ministers who have responsibility at the national level. As a result, it establishes guidelines that are hardly different from current national policies. Moreover, in many countries, the budgetary authority is effectively in the hands of the Parliament, which may make it hard for ministers meeting in the Council to take fiscal policy commitments. The Commission has the institutional independence to propose a view of how national policies ought, in its judgement, to evolve in the framework of a co-ordinated and consistent approach. But the Council cannot be expected, as a matter of regular procedures running twice or three times per year, to adopt alternative views of national economic policy.

The economic policy issue concerns the place of short-run and demand-side adjustments of budgetary policy. The 1974 Convergence Decision is clearly looking dated in relation to currently favoured views of how economic policy should best be managed. The frequency of procedural commitments in the texts is, at least as regards budgetary policy, in line with ideas of fine-tuning of the economy that were favoured over a decade ago.

In recent years, there has been a profound change of priorities in budgetary policy, with much increased emphasis on medium-term and supply-side objectives for the main taxation, public expenditure and public debt aggregates. The cross-country impact of these strategic aspects of budgetary policy may be less immediate than its short-run and demand-side aspects. None the less, there are still issues of common interest involved in the time-path and speed with which the major European countries implement such strategies, and the Economic Policy Committee of the Community has a role to play in evaluating these. Moreover, the adequacy of mechanisms in the budget for automatic cyclical stabilization should not be neglected.

Constitutional regimes should, of course, accommodate a sufficiently wide range of political and economic conditions. They should certainly not be designed for fashions in economic thinking or ephemeral circumstances. In criticizing the Convergence Decision for its dated view of fine-tuning of budgetary policy, the Group would not wish to go to the other extreme and argue that the system should not envisage circumstances calling for co-ordinated adjustments of budgetary policy. The Group considers that some interpretations of the Concerted Action decided at the Bonn Summit in 1978 have been excessively critical.

A positive outcome of the Convergence Decision has been the production, in the Annual Economic Report, of a substantial reference document which combines several roles: presentation of economic forecasts on a consistent basis, an integrated view of economic policy at national and Community levels, including micro- as well as macroeconomic policies, and an attempt to define a common strategy in relation to common policies. Thus the last two Reports [36,37] have outlined a Co-operative Growth Strategy with a view to reducing unemployment substantially by the end of the decade.

The idea reflected in the 1974 Convergence Decision of a continuous overlay of Community guidelines for national budgetary policies is implausible for constitutional as well as economic policy reasons, as mentioned. However, the opposite position, of rejecting a priori that co-ordinated actions may at times be called for, or arguing that budgetary policy adjustments can have no useful real impact on the economy would also be mistaken and dangerous. In highly interdependent economies unco-ordinated economic policies can drift into systematic deflationary bias. The international coherence of medium-term budgetary strategies and questions of time-path in their implementation require deeper attention in the relevant Community bodies.

9
Community Budget Functions

The Community budget for 1987 amounts to 37 billion ECUs, equivalent to 1 per cent of GDP. Two-thirds of this expenditure supports the Common Agricultural Policy. The remainder is distributed among several policy functions (regional, social, energy, industrial, research, fisheries, development aid), most of which are funded only to a small degree by the Community compared with national budgets. Comprehensive descriptions of the budget's mechanisms are available elsewhere [20, 21].

The budget is funded about one-third by customs duties and agricultural levies, and two-thirds by a share of value-added tax revenues. The latter are currently being drawn upon at their maximum level authorized by Treaty legislation, namely 1.4 per cent of the harmonized value-added tax base. In fact, the effective rate of value-added tax revenues is somewhat less because the United Kingdom and Germany contribute at less than 1.4 per cent as part of the agreements reached to correct budgetary imbalances between Member States.

The budget is authorized in a legislative process involving the Commission, Council, and Parliament. The Council has the last word as regards the larger part of the budget, including notably the agricultural fund. However, the Parliament has limited powers of final decision for some other domains of expenditure (categorized as 'non-obligatory', and notably excluding agricultural expenditure) within the constraint of a maximum rate of growth determined by reference to certain macroeconomic aggregates (essentially, nominal GDP and budgetary expenditures of the Member States on average). Conciliation procedures also exist, enabling the Council and Parliament to act jointly when they so agree.

There are problems of political control and policy design in the Community budget. Before turning to these, it should be noted that the main functions of the Community budget can be quite justified at the level of primary systemic choices. Following from decisions to have open agricultural trade combined with market intervention to assure price stability, common control and funding of the intervention mechanisms is logical; indeed, necessary because of impossible problems of externalities and co-ordination in the hypothesis of national intervention. The Social Fund was introduced to ease labour market adjustment problems associated with structural changes following from the opening of markets. Similarly, the Regional Fund was introduced to ease the regional adjustment problems of market integration. Research expenditure is directed towards projects having supra-national economies of scale or contributing to common strategic industrial policies such as in information technology. On the revenue side, the transfer of customs duties and agricultural levies to the Community budget is equally logical, since the point of entry of imports into the Community is no sound guide to where the tax burden is borne.

The main systemic problems of the Community budget are (a) serious problems in the decision-making system regarding the control of agricultural spending; (b) complementary problems of 'tokenism' in the scale of intervention in the case, for example, of regional and labour market policies, and a consequential weakening of their possible impact in relation to the policy objectives in question; (c) distributional problems between Member States, which have been settled only at very high costs of negotiation and confusion of purpose; and (d) tensions over the distribution of powers between the Council and Parliament, which at times override concern for the substantive policy functions in question. There have none the less been some positive developments, for example in successive adaptations of the Regional Fund and introduction in 1986 of the Integrated Mediterranean Programmes: both of these instruments have seen moves in the direction of improved incentive mechanisms, and less recourse to quota allocation methods which undermine the incentives to national or regional authorities.

The problem of controlling agricultural spending is a common factor linking these four issues. The agricultural policy is at present generating other negative consequences—for example, a cost to the Community in its external trade relations with the rest of the world.

With the successive enlargements of the Community, these various problems have become increasingly acute. As regards the United Kingdom, the budget burden-sharing issue has predominated. As regards the new Mediterranean Member States, the main issue would seem rather to be whether the Community is to be properly equipped to help the adjustment and development problems of the peripheral and least-prosperous regions, alongside its determination to open markets and increase competition. The years since the first Community enlargement have also seen a spreading of regional problems to many older industrial and urban centres, and completion of the internal market may further intensify the scale of the adjustment problems in some of these areas. These factors point to the need for substantial changes in the way the Community budget is structured and managed, and this is discussed in a later section.

The Community budget needs to be seriously reformed, as recognized in recent proposals of the Commission [22]. *There are important functions that need to be built up, such as financing industrial research and development and aiding convergence and reconversion efforts of backward and industrially declining regions. Moreover, agricultural spending has to be controlled firmly, and equity problems resolved.* These issues are returned to in Chapter 12.

PART D

TOWARDS A BALANCED DEVELOPMENT OF THE COMMUNITY SYSTEM

10
Rethinking the System

The foregoing chapters reviewed the Community's main policies according to familiar sectoral headings. This revealed a mixed pattern—of achievement and regress, of innovation and stagnation, and of more and less successful adaptation of the institutions to evolving circumstances.

The next chapters look to the future. They will go into some detail, so as to be reasonably concrete. However, the Group's first concern is to make a correct diagnosis of the essential problems, and to identify the broad directions along which solutions are to be sought. The details of proposals may then be read as being illustrative rather than definitive. The main point will be to consider the Community system as a whole and to outline the proposed actions as interrelated parts of a single strategy.

Past and present problems. What is striking about any broad review of the Community's policy-making activities is the enormity and complexity of the range of policies over which the Community is apparently called upon to act. The Community was given in its early years a model in which policy functions were, one after the other, to be transferred from the Member States to the Community. Coal, steel, trade, agriculture did follow one after the other. Elements of other policies also developed: competition, industry, social affairs, technology, transport, money, environment, and so on. If all of these policy responsibilities had been largely transferred to the Community institutions, the political landscape of Europe would have been transformed beyond all recognition. Ways were to be found to ensure an evolutionary rather than a revolutionary process, and, if not that, then blockage. Specialized formations of the Council limited the integration of Community policy–making. The unanimity rule prevailed, or hovered as a threat to discourage ambitious initiatives.

For some, these reactions may have overcome the threat of premature integration. However, they did so at a considerable cost. There remained considerable tensions between parts of the system still motivated by the model envisaging monolithic harmonization, and other parts mainly intent on resisting these features. The segmentation of powers between the several specialized Councils of Ministers led in some degree to policy-making by interest-groups, each armed with veto powers, and weakened the possibility for coherence between different policies. The European Council could only partly overcome these problems.

The illustration of these problems was presumably clear enough in the foregoing chapters: too many sectoral policies that reverted to market segmentation or prevented market opening; harmonization ambitions that overreached plausible limits; legal powers inadequately backed by the means of implementation; policy designs that became long on procedures and short in substance.

Contrasting with these formidable problems, recent years have none the less seen some promising new directions in the Community's development. Several of them, all of systemic importance, may be recalled. The European Monetary System has broadly succeeded in terms of its substantive policy objectives, while relying upon some particular institutional innovations—'variable geometry' membership and a *sui generis* model of co-ordination of national authorities. The rebirth of a radical internal market concept in 1985 has shown the Community political system to be capable in principle of responding to a strategic challenge. The combination of the mutual recognition principle on the one hand, and more majority-voting in the Council on the other, has shown also a capacity of healthy institutional evolution.

However, these innovations, while extremely important, do not yet ensure a comprehensive strategy for a balanced evolution of the Community economic system. There are still a set of *ad hoc* moves, not a policy covering the various aspects of the Community in a consistent and systematic way.

Future directions. In the search for a systematic rather than *ad hoc* approach, the group has retained for the following chapters the familiar triple distinction between the *allocation, stabilization and distribution* branches of public policy. The distinction is in some degree artificial, since the functions are far from being wholly separate in practice. However, its great advantage is to facilitate discussion of the strategic interrelations between the major policy functions that are the Community's concern. It provides the means of appraising where this or that major policy objective needs to be balanced with other initiatives elsewhere in the system. In fact, systems of government at all levels have to achieve a certain balance in their attention to the three functions. This can be seen at the world level in the GATT, IMF, and IBRD—three institutions which approximate to the allocation, stabilization, and distribution functions. This is equally evident in the Community, with its market policies, the EMS and the structural funds, and the EIB (European Investment Bank).

In proceeding in the next chapter with the allocation function, it is noted that a vast amount of microeconomic legislation to liberalize markets should lead to an improvement in the macroeconomic rate of potential economic growth. This is a major goal indeed. However, it raises several further issues in consequence. If there is to be a vast amount of detailed legislation, what problems of implementation and surveillance will follow? What are the institutional implications of this? If the cumulative impact is to be of macroeconomic significance, what does this effectively mean for macroeconomic policy, and what distributional issues will arise?

As regards the monetary stabilization function, it will be argued (and on this issue economists enjoy a virtual consensus) that the complete opening of capital markets will qualitatively change the operating environment for monetary policy convergence. This in turn makes it necessary to examine the consequences for the evolution of the European Monetary System. The status quo will no longer suffice.

As regards the budgetary and distribution function, the starting situation is one requiring in the first place serious reform of the Community budget. This will involve securing effective control of agricultural spending, and designing a revised set of budgetary mechanisms that will avoid endemic conflicts over issues of budgetary equity. However, success in these respects will require in all likelihood changes in systems, either in decision-making systems or the mechanisms of policy. With these prerequisites satisfied, the Community's budget will be able to concentrate on two important tasks that complement the internal market programme: the funding of technology and research, so as to balance the opening of market opportunities with actions to make good strategic weaknesses in the Community's world competitiveness; and the supporting of regional development and reconversion programmes so as to ensure that even the least-favoured parts of the Community economy can reasonably profit from the total impact of its policies.

Overall, it is the Group's judgement that the Community's present initiatives in the allocation branch do indeed need to be balanced by policy developments in the stabilization and distribution branches. Such balance is required not so much to enlarge the competence of the Community for its own sake, but to ensure the success of the 'allocation programme' implicit in the decision to enlarge the membership of the Community to Spain and Portugal and to create a market without internal frontiers by 1992. Indeed, if no action is taken in these areas, even the *acquis* in other fields would be at stake.

11

The Internal Market as a Strategy for Efficient Resource Allocation

Only some selected issues are now raised concerning the internal market programme itself. This is because the completion of the market by 1992 is a political premise for the Group's work, and because the Group strongly endorses the programme as a potential source of great economic advantages. The 1992 objective should not be put into doubt.

11.1 Which priorities?

While the White Paper [1] contains a formidable agenda for legislative action, there are several important requirements for achieving the market without frontiers that it hardly deals with. These omissions include the problem of monetary compensatory amounts in agriculture, and national quotas in steel, textiles, and milk products. The disadvantages of quota regimes must be underlined. They freeze economic structures and create situations of economic rent. They may also be inimical to the concept of cohesion, since the new and poorer Member States may have comparative advantages for some of these products, and should have opportunities to improve their market shares. The progressive removal of these quasi-tariffs (in agriculture) and phasing out of quota systems thus deserves a high priority, recognizing however that such reforms may be very difficult to implement.

The White Paper itself lists over three hundred items of Community legislation required to complete the internal market. No one suggests that all are equally important, but none the less, a score-card is kept in these simple quantitative terms. For example, the Commission reported to the European Council meeting towards the end of 1986 that there were 134 proposals due to have been adopted by the Council by the end of 1986. Of these, about 50 were in fact adopted before the year end, leaving over half of the scheduled total unadopted. The Commission judged this progress to be 'disappointing'.

Given the ambitious scale of the programme, it becomes necessary to reflect on priorities, so as to decide which questions warrant attention at the highest political level.

The problem of the legislative burden of the White Paper points to questions of harmonization strategy. In fact, a change in the Community's doctrine on harmonization has been under way for some years. The era of absurdities appears to have passed away—with the demise, for example, of notorious proposals for harmonizing the time of day during which lawnmowers could be used, or what could be legally described as ice-cream or chocolate.

By officially adopting the principle of *mutual recognition* suggested by the White Paper, the Community has accomplished a most important change in its market integration strategy and reopened the way for effective dismantling of non-tariff barriers. The White Paper marks the transition from a mono-lithic conception of the Community's integration process, in which national legislation and powers are replaced by Community powers, to a pluralistic, pragmatic, and federalistic conception in which national legislation will not be replaced but framed in a way that respects minimum Community requirements. This new strategy is consistent with a more general principle, that of subsidiarity (see Chapter 2), according to which the higher level of government should only take on functions that deliver public goods that cannot be effectively provided by a lower level of government. The list of such public goods would certainly include unrestricted access of all suppliers to the common market, minimum safety and stability standards, minimum con-sumer and investor protection. Thus, the Community should only be active where it alone can deliver Community-level public goods.

The mutual recognition principle was already referred to in the Treaty of Rome in the context of professional qualifications, and introduced relatively early in the financial sector. It began to be used widely in the technical standards field in the early 1980s. However, the White Paper generalized the principle and spelt out the philosophy behind it. It is the Group's strong belief that further movement in this decentralizing direction is both desirable and necessary if the objective of 1992 is to be met.

The essence and value of the principle of mutual recognition have been emphasized by Giersch [15] with what he calls '*competition among rules*'. According to this view, it will be beneficial to the economy for there to be competition not only between the producers of goods and services, but also between governments in the specification of many regulations governing production and trade. Indeed, beyond regulations governing very basic safety conditions or where intense external effects are caused in trading conditions, it is preferable for governments to be free to experiment. Consumers will become informed about different product qualities, and where regulations are ineffici-ently specified or excessively burdensome, producers in those jurisdictions will lose market share; the authorities will be induced to reconsider their regulations. Many domains of microeconomic policy may be concerned—for example, technical standards for goods; subsidies; prudential standards for financial services; and the rules of taxation.

The Group supports the view that it is wrong in principle for areas of commerce to be opened only if and when the regulatory costs imposed by different governments are equivalent. (This argument is frequently used in the Council of Ministers for blocking competition-opening proposals.) The insurance market is a case in point. Countries blocking the opening of this market point to their 'superior' prudential requirements, when it may be truer to point simply to 'higher regulatory costs'. The Community should establish minimum regulatory requirements, and allow the market to determine the value of more costly regulatory standards as revealed by the gain or loss of market shares.

Another important area of application of these principles is taxation and subsidization. For taxation the point concerns the degree of approximation of indirect tax rates best required before frontiers are abolished. Tax differences presumably accord with different social and political preferences, and with open frontiers this may lead to various revenue gains and losses as a result of cross-frontier shopping. There should be room for the trade-off between these different social preferences and revenue gains and losses to be made freely in the light of experience, rather than pre-negotiated in ways that become rigidly fixed. It would be natural, moreover, for different frontiers to cause different amounts of revenue gains and losses. Greece, Ireland, and the United Kingdom, for example, have no land frontiers with the rest of the Community, and the optimal degree of fiscal differentiation in these cases would normally be higher than around the French–German–Benelux frontiers, always supposing no fiscal frontiers. The objective of abolishing fiscal frontiers has to be strongly suggested, but this may be done with different degrees of fiscal harmonization. (The Commission is due soon to publish its detailed proposals for indirect tax harmonization, and the Group does not attempt to anticipate their content.)

Similarly on subsidies (discussed more fully in the next section): there should be a clear distinction between the question of efficient versus inefficient subsidy policies, on the one hand, and the question of what should or should not enter into the Community jurisdiction. Only when there are sharp impacts on trading conditions across frontiers should subsidies be a matter of Community jurisdiction. Otherwise, countries should be free to experiment and draw their own conclusions. Consultative bodies in the Community such as the Economic Policy Committee may usefully prepare policy analyses and opinions in such cases, but this kind of activity should be clearly distinguished from areas of legal intervention by the Community, in which issues of centralization versus decentralization of powers arise. These arguments reinforce the point already made recommending against a Community attempt at harmonization of social security.

11.2 How much competition?

The most important issue for competition policy may be put in a simple way. In the move towards abolition of all remaining frontier barriers by 1992, should competition policy at the Community level be executed more strongly or more softly? A qualified answer to this question is called for. There are arguments of a general character on both sides of the question.

The argument in favour of a stronger competition policy starts with the point that subsidies to specific firms and industries are widespread in the Community, especially taking into account covert subsidies in the shape of state participation in the equity of firms that are unprofitable. Steel, ships, cars, computers, and air transport are some of the major examples among tradeable products. The larger part of the benefits from opening the internal market can only be achieved through the increase in competition—the reduction in prices and rationalization of less efficient producers. Without this, there can hardly be any gains at all. It would be contradictory to allow more subsidies and cartelistic practices with one hand, while eliminating trading barriers with the other. However, the argument goes further than this. There is evidence, observed in the behaviour of firms and markets, that for the full benefits to be achieved from removal of market barriers it is necessary for firms to *expect* to be competing on fair terms against other firms, not against governments who might enter the field if their firms were seriously losing market share. The evidence, revealed by the price differentials that remain between open markets, is that firms hold back on actively competitive market strategies when they believe that governments might be provoked into entering the field [23]. It is more advantageous, in these circumstances, to take higher profits on lower sales. This is as damaging to the process of obtaining gains from trade as are formal barriers. There has to be a widely perceived confidence in the conditions for open competition, and this confidence is probably not of a high order at present given the extent of governmental subsidies. Since the internal market programme will surely also create more demands for subsidies, it is necessary to be armed more resolutely to enforce conditions of competition.

The counter-argument is that from an economic point of view, subsidies amount to making a gift to foreign purchasers and will therefore in the end be self-defeating and self-disciplined. Thus, in this view, external controls are not needed. Moreover, from a political point of view, the internal market programme will eliminate or restrain a number of the present prerogatives of national administrations. Detailed microeconomic policy actions of a regulatory or financial character are the means whereby government responds to demands for solutions to problems. Scope for 'positive' action by national governments is to be reduced under many of the headings of the internal market. Therefore some wider room for manœuvre needs to be handed back, for example as regards state subsidies, for the overall internal market-opening process to be plausibly balanced from a political point of view [24].

Both arguments are important, and principles are needed to conciliate them. The dominant principle should be the geographic extent of the market affected. Where the impact is only local, the responsibility for control should lie correspondingly at the lowest level of government. The Community should only be concerned where the Community market is appreciably affected. As this principle may in practice not be directly applicable, some more operational rules, approximating to this principle, have to be used. We shall consider state subsidies first, and market and company behaviour second.

In the area of state aid, greater selectivity in Community intervention could both increase the effectiveness of, and reduce the tensions generated by Community interventions. One such approach involves the question of the desirable level of detail or size of state subsidies with which the Community should be concerned. The Commission has in recent years made increasing use of *threshold criteria* for excluding from full notification and examination procedures minor aid schemes falling below certain limits that relate to the size of the enterprise (100 employees), intensity of the aid (2,000 ECUs per job created), or total amount of aid in a given scheme (0.2 million ECUs). It is also the case that the Commission's competition department finds itself seriously overloaded (thirty-five officials of administrative grade work on the control of all state subsidies). While these staff resources are not large, the combination of the political argument just mentioned and the practical problems of controlling a vast number of national aid schemes both point in the direction of allowing more small aid schemes to pass under thresholds. Below such thresholds, national schemes may not only be subject to simplified procedures, they could be formally excluded from Community jurisdiction.

A second policy orientation that can help in this task of reconciliation is the distinction between subsidies of general or very diffuse application in the economy, versus those of firm- or sector-specific application. This distinction has always been fundamental in Community competition policy, and this distinction is appropriate. Various aids of a general character may be wise or unwise economic policy, but the Member States have to make this judgement. The fact that such subsidies are of wide application makes the process of self-discipline within countries more likely. However, recognition of the borderline between general (admissible) aid and specific (inadmissible, distorting) aid is at times unclear, and there is probably a degree here also of flexibility that the Commission can exploit without undermining its essential responsibilities.

A third category of subsidy in this connection is that of *regional aid*. Community competition policy limits the grant element of regional aid according to a map which, within countries, identifies the severity of regional handicaps. The range of maximum permissible grant elements is between 10 per cent of the investment cost for the most central regions to 75 per cent in the case of Ireland, Portugal, and parts of Spain and Greece. The Community is currently discussing with its new Member States their regional subsidy schemes, whose actual grant elements could soon be effectively raised, in the case of Portugal and Spain, from 30 per cent to 75 per cent. Community grants from the Regional Fund will in part fund these important increases. This increased margin for subsidizing new investment, alongside Social Fund aid for vocational training and retraining, should be understood as a counterpart to Community disciplines over other subsidies which may be both trade-distorting and detrimental to structural adjustment.

As regards Community *competition policy addressed to private companies*, two issues deserve attention: mergers and co-operation agreements between firms. With respect to the prior notification of mergers and their prevention where necessary, the Community's competition policy instruments have been weaker than those of the United States anti-trust policy and some Member States. Community law only allows actions to be taken ex-post where the abuse of dominant market positions is determined. The Commission proposed already in 1973 a regulation that would require prior notification to the Community of mergers and concentrations above a certain size. This proposal was modified in 1981 and 1984 but remains unadopted by the Council. Given the increasing irrelevance of merger policy controls at the level of individual Member States, a proposal of this kind would now be timely at the Community level in the context of internal market integration. Consideration may be given to this merger-control function being devolved to an independent Community institution, following the model of the German federal cartel office.

With respect to inter-firm co-operative agreements, the Community in 1984 relaxed the prior rules in order to allow firms to co-operate on R&D, and to extend such co-operation to the production and marketing of products. This represents a considerable relaxation of competition policy in the interests of a strategic policy objectives [23].

Overall, the time seems ripe for a thorough review of Community competition policy, covering both state subsidies and policy towards market behaviour of private companies. The effectiveness of competition policy in the Community needs to be strengthened in the context of the internal market programme, but this should be done in ways that focus more selectively on the cases of greatest importance to the Community market, with lesser intervention wherever only national or local markets are mainly affected. The political independence of the executive and judiciary in Community competition policy need absolutely to be maintained. An appropriate formula should be identified to improve the operational effectiveness of a stronger but duly selective competition policy.

11.3 Measures to favour European enterprise

One of the striking differences between the economic areas of the European Community and the United States is the sense in which in the United States many of the leading industrial and commercial interests can hardly be identified with individual states or regions. This is clearly not yet the case in Europe, and the few multinational enterprises with diffuse European identities are exceptional. The identity of enterprises in this sense has many aspects, including share ownership and other sources of capital, the location of investment and sourcing of inputs, and the nature of business strategies.

The formation of European enterprises is of strategic importance for exploiting the potential benefits of the Community's internal market. This is both for economic and political reasons. On the economic side, the fully integrated market will naturally favour the emergence of enterprises capable of exploiting the economies of scale offered by a market of 320 million consumers. However, such enterprises will often have to be very finely adapted to a wide spread of local market preferences, or of specialized resources: they will often therefore need complex European structures. On the political side, there is the important task of favouring the acceptance of market-opening, and competition-enhancing policies. This acceptance will be greatly hindered if the process becomes one of gladiatorial contests between 'national champions', in which the winner takes all. Development of European enterprise is thus to be desired not only as an end, but also as a means of achieving a fully integrated European market. However, this process will surely be a much deeper process than seen in the (often unsuccessful) experiences of 'marriages' between national champions.

Some of the major prerequisites for the emergence of European enterprise are discussed elsewhere in this report, notably the basic freedoms for the movement of goods and services and the factors of production. All of these freedoms are fundamental. The following paragraphs therefore add further elements, in which several more precise and 'positive' policies can be deployed to encourage the emergence of European enterprise, complementing the largely 'negative' policies ('negative' in the sense of removing obstacles rather than introducing incentives) discussed elsewhere [24].

Two categories of monopoly situations call for special attention. First is the case in which the Community is faced by the threat of a world-wide monopoly or oligopoly, controlled entirely by third countries. Second is the opposite case, in which efficiency in some sectors of the Community economy is hampered by the existence of a set of deeply entrenched national monopolies. The former category is illustrated by the place of the United States in civilian aircraft manufacture in the early 1970s. The second category is illustrated by some equipment goods industries whose markets are largely in government procurement: an example is the manufacture of railway locomotives—a highly tradable commodity in which there is very little intra-Community trade.

The first category identifies conditions under which derogations from normal rules of concentration and state subsidy policies may work in the economic interest of the economy in question. Where foreign companies establish *world monopolies or oligopolies*, the non-producing economy buys at prices that may include super-profits and/or reflect higher than optimal costs. In this case, the economy that faces the world monopoly or oligopoly may find it less costly to organize its own competitor than normal principles of competition policy would at first sight suggest. In particular, a strategic government commitment to a competing industrial enterprise, for example of the Airbus type, may have a powerful effect on the behaviour of the producer in a third country, who might otherwise become a monopoly. The cost of protecting the domestic competitor may be significantly offset in the lower price of supplies from the foreign dominant producer, notably where the foreign producer achieves a substantial market share in any case [23]. Similar arguments apply also to military aircraft, a field in which collaborative ventures have multiplied in recent years with support from the IEPG (Independent European Programme Group) of NATO [25].

The second category, the problem of *too many national champions*, is often associated with questions of government procurement and state ownership. Where the buyer is the public sector and there are few, or only one national seller, possibly state-owned, it is extremely difficult to enforce the introduction of competition by initiatives purely at the level of Community law. This is illustrated by the current task of extending competition rules to the so-far 'excluded sectors' of government procurement, such as transport and energy-generating equipment. The problem of liberalizing civil aviation is also aggravated by the state ownership of many leading airlines.

These problems of market failure may be handled in different ways. Indeed, there are two distinct issues: (a) the existence of bilateral monopolies in single countries (both buyer and seller are monopolies); and (b) the question of state ownership and privatization.

Where the starting situation is one with deeply entrenched *bilateral monopolies* (as seen with railway equipment, telecommunications and energy equipment), the public authorities may have a role to play in favouring the strategic reorganization of the industries concerned. At the level of the suppliers, this may well involve the formation of new European industrial groups. There are signs that this may be happening now in telecommunications equipment. The need for it in railway equipment too is evident, but progress less so.

The current trend towards *privatization* of state enterprises introduces a new element of flexibility in this situation. Privatization programmes in the Community presently contain examples of both buyers of equipment (airlines, telecommunications agencies) and producers (aircraft, telecommunications equipment, etc.). Privatization programmes have not so far been much motivated by European market considerations. However, this aspect deserves to be considered more actively. Privatization will often offer more chances of flexible regroupings of industrial structure. Also, however, the sale of large amounts of share capital offers opportunities for creating diffuse European share-holding interests, which, as pointed out above, should be part of the process of favouring European enterprise.

The Community's subsidization of *pre-competitive research and development* in the technologies of fast-growing industries forms part of the range of instruments suitable for encouraging the emergence of European enterprise. The initial programme of this type concerned information technologies (ESPRIT), and the model is being widened for telecommunications (RACE)

and new industrial materials (BRITE). These programmes require collaborative R&D efforts between enterprises of more than one Community
country. The idea is not only to exploit potential economies of scale in the
narrow sense of laboratory research work, but also to induce management to
become involved in trans-European strategies at the earliest stage of the
product cycle.

The question of integration of the Community's policies for technology and
for the regional distribution of economic activity is also an important issue.
Technology policy must as a first priority aim at a stronger competitive
position of the Community *vis-à-vis* other industrialized powers. Efficiency
considerations must therefore be paramount. However, the diffusion of
advances in modern technology throughout the Community should also be a
policy objective, with a view to helping less-favoured regions overcome their
economic handicaps.

A common corporate tax system. The most important aspect of harmonization in
this area should be the corporate tax base not the rates of tax. Previous
attempts by the Community to harmonize corporate taxes focused almost
exclusively on the tax treatment of dividends, and in particular flows of
dividends across national frontiers. But differences in tax rates can exist, as in
the US, and will be limited by competition between revenue authorities in any
case. It is the base of the corporate tax that is crucial.

We see many advantages, as set out in Annex B, in moving to a system in
which companies are taxed on the basis of their cash flow. *A cash-flow
corporation tax* would eliminate distortions between different types of investment and different methods of financing. Concern about such distortions was
part of the motive for the restructuring of the corporate tax systems in the UK
in 1984 and the US in 1986. In both cases, the rate of tax was cut and
allowances for investment reduced. But these developments raise at least as
many questions as they answer. The calculation of economic depreciation and
indexation of the corporate tax system, both of which are necessary for a
satisfactory income-based approach, are difficult to implement in practice. An
alternative approach based on the taxation of corporate cash flow seems more
likely to offer the prospect of a stable solution. While the details of this
proposal are explained elsewhere [26], the principle is that companies would
be taxed on the net cash flow received from their real business activities. The
tax base would be the difference between the receipts from sales of goods and
services and the purchases of all real goods and services required in the
production process, including the purchases of capital goods. No distinction is
made between capital and income in the calculation of a company's tax base.
By basing the tax on cash flow, the measurement of economic income is
removed from the concern of the tax authorities. Such a system achieves fiscal
neutrality by harmonizing investment incentives on a common basis, namely,
immediate expensing of all investment expenditure. A tax base of this kind
can also cope more easily with exchange rate gains and losses which have

posed problems for tax authorities in recent years. It also puts investment in plant and equipment on the same footing as investment in R&D.

The implementation of a cash-flow tax system would involve certain transitional problems for public budgets, but these would not be greater than those absorbed in many earlier tax reforms.

11.4 The emerging compliance problem and institutional issues in the area of market policies

The explosive growth of infringement proceedings, involving cases where the Commission has had to initiate formal action over problems of non-compliance with Community law, is portrayed graphically in Fig. 11.1. This shows that until the early 1970s, the number of such cases was small or moderate. Since then the number of cases, at all levels of the legal procedures, has grown

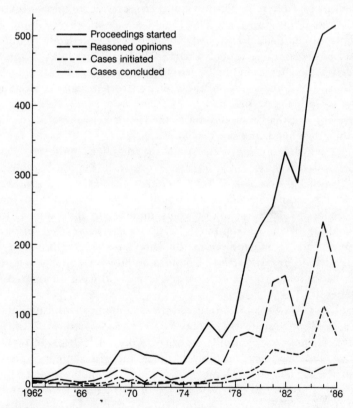

Source: Legal Service of the European Commission.

FIG. 11.1   Number of infringement proceedings under community law

enormously, to the point that the resources of the relevant services of the Commission and of the Court of Justice are seriously strained. As a result, the queues of unresolved cases have grown longer. It is also safe to assume that the compliance problem is greater than the number of infringement proceedings indicates. This is a worrying sign for reputation and efficiency of the Community's system of law, which has in itself been one of the most remarkable features of the Community integration process [27]. The Community is in its system of law much more institutionally developed than in the domains, for example, of economic or foreign policy co-operation. This is seen in the primacy and direct application of Community law in its domains of jurisdiction, and the role of the Court of Justice as a final arbiter on issues of Community law.

There are several new developments that will affect the emerging compliance problem, some of which will ease the situation, some accentuate it.

The positive developments are, first, the increased emphasis given to the mutual recognition principle in the White Paper, which means that there will in such cases be more room for national preferences in the implementation of general Community directives. This should reduce the probabilities of non-compliance by national authorities. Second, there is the likely creation of a 'tribunal of first instance' at the Court of Justice. (Art. 140A of the Single European Act in effect contains an invitation to the Court of Justice to request establishment of a lower level to the Court to treat certain classes of actions brought by private parties.) Such an innovation could well help relieve pressures both on the Commission and the Court of Justice at its top level.

On the other hand, the sheer mass of legislation called for by the White Paper will unavoidably add to the size of the compliance problem, even with more mutual recognition. The greater recourse to majority voting in the Council, while a necessary act to facilitate the legislative process, may translate in some degree into greater problems of compliance in countries which found themselves in the outvoted minority in the Council. Indeed, some analysts of the Community's legal system judge that institutional problems already lie much more on the compliance side, rather than that of the legislative: 'time lags between Commission proposal and Council decision seem to be shortening ..., and backlogs ... seem to have diminished rather than increased' [27].

A traditional view has been to regard the Community's institutional system in terms of Montesquieu's trichotomy between the legislative (Council), the executive (Commission), and the judiciary (Court of Justice). In reality, the legislative and executive function is much more a shared responsibility between the Commission, Member States, and emanations of the Council such as the COREPER (the Committee of Permanent Representatives of Member States). The volume of Community legislation is now such that more resources are going to have to be applied to ensure compliance. The Commission's resources are in reality quite small, notably for competition and external and internal market policies. However, there is little wish in any part of the Community system that these resources be greatly expanded. If this is accepted, the consequences will have to be to find ways of accentuating features of Community policies which require decentralized implementation, and which mobilize the resources of national administrations and indeed the individual (through his scope for individual litigation). This should not, in the Group's judgement, be viewed as an institutionally retrograde step. It would certainly be a further move away from a monolithic model, often envisaged in the past, for the distribution of policy competences, in which given policies were to be transferred wholly from national to Community level. In a different model, which the Group feels is more plausible for the future development of the Community, there would be more domains of competences shared between the Commission and Member States in policy-making and implementation.

Examples have already been mentioned (in preceding sections) that fit into this view of how the institutions should adapt to the Community's increased ambitions for its internal market policies. The mutual recognition principle should probably be exploited even more actively. The rules of competition policy should exploit all possibilities for threshold criteria to exclude small affairs from the Community's responsibility. The rules governing the complex structure of official committees of Commission and Member States representatives should allow for special cases in which there could be shared responsibilities for formulating in detail and implementing policies where these functions cannot be separated in a categorical way. The general rules of the institutions need to provide increasingly for democratic accountability, which such Committees will typically not satisfy. However, the domain of regulation of financial institutions, which link to the responsibilities of central banking functions, provides a clear example where the old monolithic model of Community harmonization and Commission executive responsibilities is implausible. (The role of the Monetary Committee and Committee of Governors of Central Banks is raised in the next chapter). Consideration should be given to identifying ways in which the reserve resource of potential litigation by the individual, using national courts before (or without) reaching Community courts, might be mobilized more fully to relieve the resources of the Commission from an unrealistically large policing role. This is especially relevant in the field of competition policy. Finally, the Commission should also, in many of its executive functions, be given greater room for exercising managerial responsibility where this is appropriate. (Examples concerning the structural funds will be given in section 12.3.) These different trends or innovations would point to the need for a pluralistic system of institutional arrangements in the Community.

12

Capital Mobility, the European Monetary System, and the Stabilization Function

12.1 Monetary stability and integration

12.1.1 Capital liberalization and monetary regime choices

The Community's strategic objective in the monetary domain is to combine the opening of capital markets with increasing convergence and ultimately monetary union.

Capital market liberalization is just one component of the internal market programme. It is, however, a component that has particularly sharp implications for other parts of the Community system, and the European Monetary System in particular. In passing from a regime of capital restrictions to one of capital mobility, more binding constraints of policy consistency will have to be respected if the EMS is to function effectively.

The addition of capital mobility to a fixed exchange rate system fundamentally changes the operating conditions for monetary and budgetary policies. The problems are not very different for a small economy linked through its exchange rate to a large economy, and for a group of countries of comparable size.

With perfect capital mobility and fixed exchange rates, interest rates in a small country will essentially be determined by those prevailing in the 'outside world'. If the central bank in the small country carried out an expansionary policy leading to an incipient decline in interest rates, there would be capital outflows and reserve losses until money market conditions restored the initial level of interest rates. Looked at in another way, an attempt to expand domestic credit leads to offsetting capital outflows and reserve losses. Either way, the small country cannot conduct an independent monetary policy but must accept the foreign interest rate and use its domestic monetary instruments to maintain the fixed exchange rate and an acceptable level of foreign reserves.

In a group of countries of comparable size in an equilibrium situation, interest rates again have to be essentially the same in every country. This case differs from that of a small country in that individual countries can have some influence on the common interest rate level and the rate of monetary expansion. When a country in the group undertakes an expansionary open market operation, it will experience some loss in its reserves, some domestic credit expansion, and an interest rate decline. The other countries will also share in this result, since capital inflows will lead to some decline in interest rates and some increase in domestic credit expansion. If the partner countries decide to counter the initial impulse by tightening monetary conditions, and the initiating country again takes offsetting action in response, then the system can become unstable. At some point, conflicting central bank actions will result in some country suffering unsustainable reserve losses or failing to maintain its exchange rate commitment. Unless agreement can be reached on the desirable level of interest rates, the system of fixed exchange rates will not hold.

These are obviously simplified examples, and the above propositions are more complex and qualified if capital is not perfectly mobile and exchange rates are not rigidly fixed [28]. The important conclusion is that a regime of open capital markets and fixed exchange rates has strong and inevitable implications for domestic monetary policy and also for fiscal policy. A small country must be prepared to accept the level of interest rates set in the larger partner country, together with exchange rate intervention rules, as the main determinant of its monetary conditions. Nor can such a country set any other strategic variables of monetary policy independently. A group of countries of comparable size has to find an agreement on how monetary policy is to be determined, and this can be achieved either by recognizing one country, formally or informally, as the leader of the group, or by reaching a co-operative approach in which monetary policy is established jointly.

Unwillingness to accept these political or institutional implications may lead to the abandonment of capital mobility, the rejection of the exchange rate commitment, or the application of different graduations in the degree of capital mobility and exchange rate stability.

12.1.2 *Present regime choices*

It may be useful to summarize the actual choices made by the Community countries and the other major economies with reference to the degree of freedom for exchange rate and capital movements. The United States is at one extreme, with a completely open capital market and a floating exchange rate. Japan and the United Kingdom have adopted a similar position, but have shown greater willingness to intervene to influence the exchange rate, albeit without formal target levels. Germany has an open capital market, while its exchange rate regime is divided between its commitments within the EMS and a relatively free floating relationship with the other key currencies. The dominant position of the Deutschmark within the EMS means, however, that Germany enjoys considerable independence in its monetary policy at present. The other country with a completely open capital market, the Netherlands, has been prepared, by contrast, to align its monetary policy closely with that of Germany. Its market interest rates are almost the same as those in

Germany, and the central bank discount rate is normally changed in line with that of Germany.

The other EMS countries have adopted different intermediate positions. Belgium and Denmark have fairly open capital markets, but have not always maintained fixed exchange rates against the Deutschmark; indeed, Belgium maintains a two-tier exchange rate, with the financial transaction rate allowed to diverge from the 'commercial' rate at times of foreign exchange pressure. France, Italy, and Ireland still restrict capital movements, although in varying degrees, and Italy's wider exchange rate band within the EMS gives it more room for manœuvre. Greece, Spain, and Portugal have different and generally tighter capital controls and do not participate in the EMS exchange rate mechanism, although their exchange rate policies are strongly influenced by European currency developments. Consequently, these countries have enjoyed varying degrees of monetary autonomy.

The participants in the EMS exchange rate mechanism have, of course, gained extra leeway through the periodic changes in the system's central rates. On the other hand, they have all been prepared, for the reasons described in an earlier chapter, to accept a degree of German monetary policy leadership. They have periodically adjusted their parties but, as a rule, they have not fully accommodated their inflation differentials with respect to Germany through exchange rate changes. They have thus reinforced their stabilization policies by exerting exchange rate 'pressure' on domestic price increases and strengthening the credibility of their monetary policies through their exchange rate commitments [2]. Relative exchange rate stability within the area has also preserved an open trade system, thereby also strengthening competition in all the participating countries.

This combination of *macroeconomic and trade discipline* on member countries has been the distinguishing feature of the system's performance. In the following, a distinction will be made between the 'performance' of the system and the 'mechanisms' that make this performance possible.

12.1.3 Implications of capital mobility for the EMS

To date, monetary co-ordination has mostly involved a leading country (Germany) providing the common monetary standard, with the Netherlands usually following, and the other EMS countries using the leeway provided by capital controls and the possibility of periodic exchange rate adjustments to maintain a degree of monetary autonomy. Such leeway was very limited for small countries such as Belgium and Denmark, greater for larger countries such as France and Italy.

Complete liberalization of capital movements would result in the system being required to perform the new and qualitatively different task of reconciling the monetary objectives of a group of countries of comparable size. Each would be exposed to the influence of the others. It would not be possible for one of the larger countries to pursue an independent monetary policy even for limited periods of time; and even the leading country might encounter difficulties or find it impossible to sustain a policy inconsistent with that adopted by the majority.

In principle, the exchange rate and monetary policy options going with the removal of capital market controls could be: (*a*) to maintain the status quo; (*b*) to leave the degree of monetary co-ordination unchanged and relax the EMS exchange rate constraint; (*c*) to strengthen both monetary co-ordination and the EMS mechanisms. These options need to be evaluated in the light of their ability to ensure that the 'performance' of the EMS—its basic policy function of macroeconomic and trade discipline mentioned above—is unimpaired, and preferably reinforced.

The *first option*—maintaining the status quo—would appear the easiest and least onerous of the three, but it is unlikely to work. In the past, the persistence of inflation differentials and divergences in monetary and fiscal policies have made periodic realignments of the EMS currencies inevitable (except perhaps for the special case of the Dutch guilder).

By limiting the size of speculative capital flows in the short run or by permitting wide differentials to develop between domestic and Euro-market rates, exchange and capital controls have reduced the amount of exchange market intervention and of 'defensive' interest rate changes needed to cope with expectations of a realignment. In the absence of capital controls, the amount of intervention needed would almost certainly be much greater, as the events of the days preceding the latest realignment (in January 1987) confirm. Interventions required would not only be greater but also likely to be less effective. If the market has information about the size of interventions, then in the absence of other corrective policy measures speculative movements would intensify and offset the effects of interventions. In these circumstances, substantial interest rate adjustments would be necessary to stem the capital flows, but countries might be unwilling to adopt such a policy and prefer instead to abandon the defence of the exchange rate. Thus the frequency of realignments would increase compared with the status quo.

In addition, in a world of perfect capital mobility, even when there is a high degree of convergence of monetary policies (as is the case at present), it may be possible to envisage situations of tensions in the exchange markets motivated not by divergence in the fundamentals but largely by news of an ephemeral character. This may especially be the case if the market perceives that the convergence is not quite complete.

In these circumstances, there is the risk that the vagaries of financial markets rather than the evolution of the real sector and the policy of the monetary authorities will determine the timing and the amount of a realignment. Furthermore, in a situation in which inflation rates have become lower and more convergent than ever before during the last fifteen years, the acceptance of an unqualified disinflationary priority and German leadership as a way to co-ordinate monetary policies is likely to decrease.

Under the 'status quo' option, there is thus a danger that destabilizing movements of capital would lead to more frequent and larger realignments than justified by the existing divergences in cost and price trends. If conflicts between domestic monetary management and the EMS exchange rate constraint were resolved by loosening the latter, in the end the basic disciplinary function of the EMS would be undermined and trade relationships disrupted. The loss of credibility of the EMS arrangements could eventually lead to a breakdown in the system.

The *second option*—institutionalizing greater exchange rate flexibility to preserve existing autonomy in monetary policies and/or accommodate the increased pressures in exchange markets which is likely to result from capital liberalization—is an inadequate and potentially dangerous answer to the problems posed by capital mobility. Apart from a greater use of the room for manœuvre offered by the existing narrow band, which may be welcomed, greater exchange rate flexibility could be achieved through a generalized widening of the band or more frequent realignments. Both solutions are incompatible with the disciplinary functions of the EMS if they allow exchange rates to move against real economic conditions.

As a 2.25 per cent band has proved to be adequate when inflation rate differentials between participating countries were of 10–15 percentage points, there is little reason to consider it too narrow now that such differentials have shrunk to 2 or 3 percentage points. On the other hand, if realignments caused by financial pressures were to determine divergences in real exchange rates, the credibility of the system would be undermined and further speculative movements would be incited rather than discouraged. The 'greater flexibility' option would make it more difficult, not easier, to preserve a fundamental EMS function, which is to keep exchange rates in line with real economic conditions in member countries and to exert pressure for monetary stability. Flexibility would mean in practice that lower inflation countries would at times tend to be pushed to an 'overvalued' level of their currencies and see their position in export markets seriously damaged, while other currencies would conversely tend to be pushed to an 'undervalued' level and suffer a re-ignition of inflation. Furthermore, the exploitation by certain countries of the greater flexibility to obtain competitive advantages and to sustain domestic economic activity could have a disruptive impact on intra-European relationships, with potential chain reactions of protectionist measures. To a certain extent, of course, these conclusions should also hold for the EMS countries that do not participate in the exchange rate mechanism, at least in so far as they should 'not be allowed' to make competitive devaluations.

In the light of the process of financial innovation and globalization of financial markets, the 'greater flexibility' option seems inappropriate also from the point of view of an individual country. The effectiveness of a monetary policy exclusively oriented towards a quantitative target set for a chosen national monetary aggregate is increasingly eroded by the higher substitutability between financial instruments and the growing speed at which financial transactions can be executed across countries and currencies. In these conditions, policy has to rely more on the anchor of a stable exchange rate.

The foregoing suggests that the *third option*—stronger EMS mechanisms coupled with strengthened monetary co-ordination—is the course to be followed if the basic performance of the EMS is to be preserved as capital movements are liberalized.

Strengthening EMS mechanisms and monetary co-ordination does not require achieving the final objective of the monetary union. In particular, it should not prevent exchange rates from periodically adjusting to differences in price and cost behaviour, shifts in consumer preferences, and changes in technology. Nor should it exclude a one-time movement in exchange rates that may be required at the time of full liberalization to accommodate the inevitable adjustment in the currency composition of financial wealth. What is necessary, instead, is to introduce in the existing arrangements the changes that are required to maintain the stability of the system under the new conditions created by capital mobility.

Monetary policy co-ordination now has to fit the case of the group of countries of comparable size, as described above. Two further reasons point to this conclusion. Firstly, the equality of countries of equivalent size is a deeply embedded principle in the Community (adopted for representation in institutions and weighting for voting in the Council, etc.). Secondly, the case for German monetary policy leadership within the EMS would be weakened as other large Community countries achieve very low inflation rates. As long as the credibility of these countries' policies is established, and this is a basic condition, it would be natural that monetary policy within the EMS be formulated jointly.

12.1.4 Organization of a 'Stage Two' for the EMS

It is thus necessary to discuss a possible configuration for a more highly developed EMS, a 'Stage Two' that would promote a common management of monetary policy while avoiding 'all-or-nothing' choices between full monetary union and the status quo (without capital liberalization).

There are four key features that such a 'Stage Two' should have:

1. *Monetary co-ordination.* In recent years, Community bodies and in particular the Monetary Committee, which includes Ministry of Finance and central bank representatives, have started to develop a co-operative approach to monetary target-setting. Before individual member states formally adopt their targets for the year ahead, the Committee discusses a scenario drawn up

by the Commission on the basis of projections or intermediate objectives of individual countries. In mid-year actual developments are reviewed in relation to the targets. As regards interest rates, some central banks already co-ordinate the changes in their discount rates quite tightly. In 'Stage Two', effective monetary co-ordination could build upon these arrangements. The basic requirements would be that targets of monetary policy be jointly agreed or set through a common procedure. Management of these targets, and notably responses to short-term disturbances induced by international port-folio shocks, would also have to be closely co-ordinated. To give an example, if a Community target on aggregate money supply for the whole area was agreed upon as reference for monetary policy, these rules for co-ordination would have to extend to ensuring that domestic monetary conditions in EMS countries remain consistent with realization of the aggregate target. What is important is that in the event of unexpected shifts between EMS currencies, intervention by central banks should not be sterilized. In this way, domestic credit expansion would remain on target, as would the aggregate money supply of the Community. This would also help to bring about appropriate interest rate differentials to maintain exchange rate cohesion, and reduce the need for intervention. These methods of co-ordination could be upgraded in a system that gave enhanced policy responsibilities to the relevant Community bodies. We are aware of certain difficulties that could be encountered in applying an aggregate money supply, and we shall return to them in Annex C, where principles that could provide a standard for a more explicit system of co-ordination are further discussed.

2. *EMS mechanism.*[1] Stronger defences will have to be built against speculative capital movements, since the latter's destabilizing potential is considerably increased by the opening of capital markets. 'Stronger defences' does not necessarily mean larger financing mechanisms. Rather, it should involve a more active, flexible, and symmetrical use of existing instruments, as well as greater reliance on market mechanisms to provide financing for the facilities [3]. Thus, if a currency is subject to pressures from destabilizing capital outflows and the consensus is that there is no need for a realignment, the tension should be treated as a Community problem. This may involve the conduct of co-ordinated intervention, both marginal and intramarginal, by all countries, with appropriate arrangements for the sharing of intervention burdens. The determination not to yield to unwarranted market pressures

---

[1] At present, the mechanisms of the EMS include the following credit facilities: very short-term (1 to 2 months); short-term (3 to 6 months); medium-term (3 to 5 years). As the duration of credits increases, the amounts become smaller and the conditions more restrictive. The very short-term facility is unlimited in amount, while the short-term facilities amount to 8.9 billion ECUs and the medium-term facility to 15.9 billion ECUs. Since portfolio shocks and speculative capital flows are of a short-term nature, the logical response would be to reinforce the matching lines of defence. At 45 days, the maturity of very short-term credit should normally suffice to cope with speculative movements of private capital, but could be extended as a precautionary measure; access to the short-term monetary support mechanism could be improved and its financing made more flexible (without necessarily envisaging an increase in the overall amount available).

could be made public by using Community instruments and bodies (ECU and EMCF)[2] to conduct recycling operations of net capital flows: the demand for currency diversification based on the expectation of a parity change not related to changes in fundamentals would be accommodated for the time necessary to deceive it and frustrate it. Since activation of the credit mechanisms would serve to protect a Community 'public good'—exchange rate stability—the related interest rate burden should be distributed in a more balanced way among all participating countries.

3. *Safeguard clauses.*[3] Under the Treaty of Rome, Member States may temporarily adopt protective measures, including capital controls, in case of serious difficulties with the balance of payments (Art. 108–9) or if turbulent conditions in capital markets jeopardize the latter's orderly functioning (Art. 73). In practice, these provisions have been resorted to in order to stem capital outflows. For a long period, the safeguard clause was interpreted somewhat freely, but in recent years the Community has restored a strict enforcement of these exceptional arrangements. The range of applicability and the procedure of Article 73 will have to be made flexible enough to allow Member States to counter speculative financial pressures in good time.[4] While the initiative to have recourse to safeguard clauses may come from a particular country, the decisions over restrictions, in particular over the duration of application, should become a fully collective decision, in the same way as the EMS central rates can only be changed by a common procedure. Safeguard clauses should not be used to justify protectionist policies in capital markets, and Member States should not unilaterally be able to take measures they deem advisable and then simply inform the Commission. As far as possible, restrictions should be symmetrical. In no case should they be imposed for more than a short period (3–6 months), and they should not be used to cope with the consequences of systematically 'divergent' policies or 'underlying' balance of

---

[2] The European Monetary Cooperation Fund (EMCF) handles the credit, reserve, and accounting mechanisms of the European Monetary System. Its Board of Governors is effectively the same as the Committee of Governors of the Central Banks of the European Community. Technical functions are executed through the agency of the Bank of International Settlements.

[3] Community law on capital flows is based (*a*) on Art. 67 of the EEC Treaty, which lays down that 'Member States shall progressively abolish ... all restrictions of the movement of capital ... and any discrimination based on nationality or on the place of residence of the parties or on the place where such capital is invested', and the Council Directive for the implementation of Art. 67, which spells out the liberalization obligations for the various types of financial transactions; (*b*) on Arts. 108 and 109 of the Treaty, which permit any Member State 'in difficulties or seriously threatened with difficulties as regards its balance of payments' to adopt, under Community control, the 'necessary protective measures', including restrictions on capital outflows; and (*c*) on Art. 73 of the Treaty and the related 1972 Council Directive 'on regulating international capital liquidity'.

[4] The explicit reference to balance of payments difficulties in Arts. 108 and 109 clearly makes them inappropriate for dealing with short-term tensions in the EMS caused by financial disturbances. Art. 73 provides a more appropriate framework, but the limited range of restrictions permitted by the implementation directive makes the scope of this procedure unduly narrow in the light of the intervening changes in financial markets (notably the proliferation of instruments for liquidity management). The applicability of Art. 73 should be broadened to permit in case of need effective control of capital flows of a short-term nature.

payments difficulties. One of the technical forms they could take is a tax on foreign exchange transactions.

4. *External monetary relations.* In 'Stage Two', the EMS should also play a part in international monetary relations. Indeed, it is increasingly anomalous if the Community, which has established an internal monetary order and plays quite an effective role in external trade relationships, largely fails to play its role in external monetary policy. The strengthening of monetary co-operation within the Community envisaged above could create an adequate basis for such a common policy. As external factors are likely to remain a source of intra-EMS tensions, any actions, negotiations, or arrangements affecting currency relationships with the outside should be taken jointly, using ECU–dollar or ECU–yen relationships as standards of reference, and with adequate provisions for burden-sharing within the EMS. A common European monetary position would significantly strengthen the bargaining power of Europe in monetary negotiations with the US and Japan. On the other hand, any commitment that would fall on EMS countries that have not directly or indirectly participated in its formulation would create monetary and even political tensions that would seriously undermine the EMS and hence the trade environment in Europe. In the field of international co-ordination, it would be advantageous for Europe to negotiate with the United States and Japan on economic and monetary policy as a single partner with decision-making and operational authority.

The implication of 'Stage Two' as described above need to be considered first for Community institutions, regulations, and procedures; and second, for the development of the ECU.

The policy functions inherent in 'Stage Two' call for a *reconsideration of the role of the relevant Community bodies*. At present, the decision-making structure envisages roles for the Council of Ministers (notably, in case of realignments and when conditional credit facilities are used), for the Committee of Central Bank Governors (on matters concerning the EMS Agreement and management of the EMCF, of which the Governors constitute the Board of Directors), and for the Monetary Committee (where finance ministries and central banks are represented) in all matters of monetary relevance.

In a Community that has set for itself the ultimate objective of a monetary union, it may be appropriate to devise already in 'Stage Two' a division of labour among the various Community bodies, in which the overall economic policy responsibility and the setting of central rates rests on governments, while the conduct of monetary policy and exchange rate operations are entrusted to the system of EMS central banks.

The functions outlined above for 'Stage Two' could be apportioned in the following way:

1. The Monetary Committee would retain full responsibility in the field of overall policy co-ordination and review, including, as indicated in (1) above,

the new function of jointly setting monetary policy targets. This role in policy co-ordination would continue to include the function of setting the framework for EMS realignments and the related accompanying measures. The Monetary Committee could also be empowered to decide (as a Community matter) on safeguard clauses as indicated in (3) above; the procedures for such decisions could be patterned on those presently applying for EMS realignments. Finally, the Monetary Committee would be responsible for the external monetary relations outlined in (4) above:

2. The Committee of Governors should be given responsibility for supervising the management of monetary policies and responses to short-term disturbances as outlined in (1) above. In this context, the Committee would have the power to co-ordinate interest rate changes and intervention strategies, as well as to activate the EMS facilities described in (2) above, particularly when the activation implies recycling operations based on the ECU. The performance of such functions might require the unification of the responsibilities of the Committee of Governors into the board of the EMCF, as the board is already empowered to take discretionary action in this field, for example as regards the ECU mobilization scheme.

The scope for Community action in 'Stage Two' would be enhanced by *further development of the ECU*, both in its role as an international reserve instrument and for use in coping with portfolio shocks within the system.

Diversified money and capital market instruments denominated in ECUs now exist in the private sector. Some central banks hold accounts or assets in private-market ECUs alongside their holdings of official ECUs (the counterpart of the 20 per cent of gold and dollar reserves deposited with the EMCF). At present, the private and official circuits of the ECU are separate. A natural development would be for the operating regulations of the EMS to be changed so as to link these two markets. This would enable central banks in Europe, both individually and collectively, to intervene more effectively in money and capital markets; it would also enhance the potential for use of the present ECU mobilization scheme by extending to the private market the function to provide liquidity for mobilization operations. A more developed ECU market could attract mobile capital, with potentially stabilizing effects on exchange rates, and be influenceable by the European central banks in view of common goals.

In the evolution of international monetary relationships, the ECU could play an increased role as a reserve instrument available (through the 'third holder' clause) to countries wishing to diversify out of the dollar, as the reference point of Community exchange rate and monetary policies *vis-à-vis* third currencies, and an instrument for common intervention policies in foreign exchange markets.

Within the system, the ECU's functions as a settlement and credit instrument could be extended. In particular, the development of a common policy tool could enhance the possibility of pursuing common monetary objectives. For instance, the interest rate on ECU credit granted through the EMS mechanisms could be set as a matter of discretionary policy at a discount or premium over market rates in Europe to signal—to both national authorities and private agents—the stance of the common monetary policy. With ECU transactions in private markets increasing and a closer integration of the private and official ECU markets, these interest rate decisions could eventually play a role equivalent to official rate setting at national level. A prerequisite for the ECU to take up such an increased role in Europe seems to be full coincidence between participation in the exchange rate arrangement and participation in the ECU basket, so that the value of the ECU would not be influenced by floating member currencies.

The liberalization of capital markets will have significant implications for the conduct of monetary policies also for the Community *countries that do not participate in the exchange rate mechanism of the EMS* and which impose considerable restrictions on capital movements. The elimination of exchange and capital controls will force these countries to choose between either pursuing a more flexible exchange rate policy or implementing the adjustments in macroeconomic policies required to maintain the prevailing degree of exchange rate stability. The second alternative would enable them to benefit from the macroeconomic and trade discipline emanating from exchange rate stabilization, and would also be consistent with the Community's objective of monetary integration. Nevertheless, the pace with which they can proceed towards the dual objective of capital liberalization and greater exchange rate stability will be constrained by two realities: the lack of well-developed financial markets and institutions, and, in certain cases, existing imbalances which exert pressures on their balance of payments. To overcome these constraints and opt for policies compatible with the Community objectives, these Member States may require Community support. Strengthening monetary co-operation and extending the scope of applicability of safeguard clauses (as proposed above) will also help countries which do not participate in the exchange rate mechanism in managing transitional balance of payment difficulties associated with the capital liberalization process. Furthermore, the eligibility criteria of the Community's structural funds and of the instruments for medium-term financial assistance should be broadened to allow the financing of the necessary restructuring and modernization of their financial markets and to support medium-term programmes aimed at achieving and consolidating macroeconomic stability. (This is further discussed in section 13.4.)

12.1.5 Some remarks on monetary union

The eventual implementation of monetary union has been repeatedly stated as an officially agreed objective for the Community and remains the end-point of the evolution of the Community in the monetary field. By monetary union, we understand an area using a single currency, managed by a unitary or federal central banking system. It is still possible for a monetary union to have distinct national currencies provided these currencies do not become the vehicle of distinct monetary policies.

As this report is essentially concerned with minimum changes required to successfully implement, and benefit from, full economic and financial integration in an enlarged Community by the year 1992, monetary union is not extensively discussed or proposed here; only a few remarks are offered, to put our short-run proposals in perspective.

In several respects, the monetary union is the first-best solution from an economic point of view because it offers two main advantages compared with an EMS-type exchange rate system. Firstly, the absence of exchange rate uncertainty fosters the integration and rationalization of economic activity. Where uncertainty exists, businesses require a higher rate of return on investments that will serve the union-wide market. Secondly, with countries no longer able to pursue accommodating monetary policies, private agents will be much less tempted to seek price or wage increases in the belief that the possible repercussions will be offset through devaluation, and fiscal authorities will be subject to a tighter capital market constraint. With inflation expectations · consequently being formed basically at the union level, it will be considerably easier to achieve the necessary convergence of national inflation rates.

This assumes that the monetary union has passed through the transitional period of its establishment, and that the institutional design of the new central banking system is propitious to monetary stability. Both these assumptions none the less pose serious problems.

One set of transition problems would concern states which joined the monetary union with large budget deficits and a large stock of public debt carrying high nominal rates of interest. Reform would provide the occasion and the incentive to implement a credible programme of fiscal stabilization that would be consistent with the loss of any future possibility to monetize the debt. At the moment of monetary reform, the old stock of public debt would be converted onto a new basis and the interest rate would be reduced to a level consistent with the low inflation rate expected of the new currency. This could in some degree help states with large debt burdens reduce the interest rate burden in their budgets. However, the period preceding the monetary reform, i.e. before the interest rate relief was secured, could pose a combination of serious budgetary and macroeconomic problems.

A second issue in the transition is whether wage bargaining would quickly settle down into habits compatible with a single inflation rate for the Community and a regionally balanced distribution of employment opportunities. Since cost pressures can be strongly influenced by the institutional conditions of national industrial relations systems, and changes in voluntary organizations like labour unions are extremely difficult to achieve, the organization of wage bargaining is not likely to converge under the pressure of unified rates of inflation. If this prediction were correct, a European monetary union with irreversibly fixed exchange rates would pose difficult problems for those countries whose international competitiveness in the past had depended upon periodic devaluations of their currencies. The transition cannot be simply taken for granted; this, indeed, is the main economic reason why we do not envisage an early move to fix exchange rate parities irrevocably.

As to the institutional design, a key issue is the degree of independence of the Community central banking system. Independence means that the decision-making process of money creation should be sheltered from pressures coming from economic agents, whether private or public, who suffer from large (actual or potential) imbalances between expenditures and receipts. Seen in this light, independence may be better assured in the Community than in a national environment, as long as the Community budget remains small and unexposed to structural deficits. However, independence would not be ensured by mechanically adopting, at the Community level, the statutes of a central bank that has the required autonomy in a national context. In particular institutional safeguards of independence will have to be established against pressures coming from countries with external deficits. This may be achieved through voting procedures within the new central banking system that would take into consideration the external position of member states. The Group, in favouring an independent European central banking system, draws attention to the fact that the new institutional design should adapt the requirement of independence to the special features of a multicountry system.

12.2 Other stabilization policy issues

12.2.1 The Community budgetary policy model in the long run

Given the inherent institutional fragility of proposals for better co-ordination of economic policy, and bearing in mind the ideas advanced above for a more strongly organized European Monetary System, it is appropriate to reflect also on the longer-run model for budgetary policy in the Community.

The view implicit in the 1974 Convergence Decision and other texts of that period is that national budgets would come under a progressively stronger Community influence in the course of moving towards economic and monetary union. Guidelines, initially of no legally binding force as in the Convergence Decision, would later become more effective.

This model is not supported by the experience of industrialized countries which have adopted confederal or federal forms of government. The predominant model among these countries (United States, Canada, Germany, Switzerland) is one in which the states retain independence in deciding on their borrowing as well as spending and taxation aggregates. The only example of power-sharing in relation to state budgets is the Australian federal loan council, where the federal agency is the borrowing agent for the states, and the federal authorities have a strong role in deciding the amount of borrowing by states. The German constitution has a provision whereby the federal authorities can in some conditions exert a marginal influence on state budgets, but this has never been used. In some federations, for example the United States, state constitutions lay down budget balance rules or borrowing limits, but the amendment of these constitutional rules remains a state responsibility. In the predominant model, the effective restraint on the borrowing of states is the sanction of the capital market, under conditions in which the state authorities have no powers for monetization of the public debt.

This model of decentralized market constraints on the borrowing of states seems to be far more plausible for the Community than the model of increasingly binding central guidelines. Nonetheless, this model would itself not be immune from certain risks. The relatively large size of several Community countries in relation to the aggregate means that the paradigm would be not so much like a competitive system with many agents (as in the United States with fifty or so states), but closer to an oligopoly calling for co-ordination between a small number of agents. In addition, some Community countries have rather long experiences of fiscal laxity to overcome. All of them, moreover, have large budgets incorporating comprehensive social security systems.

In the mature federations mentioned, there is a further element in the budgetary system. The federal budget tends to account for around a third to half of the transaction of all levels of government, and will typically amount to 15 to 20 per cent of GDP. This is because the federation supplies some important public goods, such as defence, justice, social security, and so on. As a result, the federal budget is of a sufficient size to allow the federal authorities to conduct a macroeconomic policy without necessarily requiring the active participation of the states. A regime of this type offers a clear allocation of responsibilities by level of government: the states are free to discharge their constitutional responsibility in certain domains of public policy. The federal authorities have exclusive macroeconomic policy powers.

For the Community in the years ahead, it may therefore be pertinent to ask whether Community finances should have a capacity for making macroeconomic policy adjustments. A proposal to move in this direction was made in 1983 by M. Albert in a report prepared for the European Parliament [30]. The model here was that the Community would for several years raise the level of its investment-financing activities (by 15 billion ECUs), with loans from the European Investment Bank and New Community Instrument, coupled to interest-rate subsidies from the Community budget (amounting to 2.5 to 5 billion ECUs per year, in turn financed by a Community oil import tax). The current budget of the Community would remain balanced, and the capital items would result in lending, not direct spending.

A second model would be for the Community's general budget to be subject to a rule of cyclical balance, allowing for deficits and surpluses over the course of a five or so year period, summing to zero. In this hypothesis, there might be an acceleration of expenditures on public investment such as transport and communication projects of common interest in a period of conjunctural weakness. Given, however, that the conceivable base of expenditures in the budget susceptible to cyclical modulation would be small, the revenue side of the budget would be the more suitable vehicle for macroeconomic policy adjustments. For this to be effective, the own resources of the general budget would have to be organized in such a way as to ensure that Community-level tax changes be directly communicated to the tax payer. The residual financing of the Community budget, within the constraints of a cyclical budget balance rule, would then be through the issuing of ECU-denominated bonds and notes. The European central banking system would be able to conduct open market operations in these assets. For such cyclical fluctuations in the community's budget balance to be of macroeconomic significance for the EC economy as a whole, their size would have to be 1 per cent of GDP as a minimum.

Such ideas are of course removed from current priorities for the Community budget. It will be argued below that to bring agricultural spending under orderly political control is a first priority. However, there is a chain of ideas whose logical implications need to be considered. If monetary integration were to move to a qualitatively more advanced level, budgetary policy at the Community level might have to extend beyond the limited potential of co-ordination.

12.2.2 Labour costs, industrial relations, and social policy

In the past, European economies have been characterized by unequal rates of inflation corresponding to national differences in the rates of increase in money supply and production costs, including unit labour costs. Under the influence of the EMS, these differences have decreased but not disappeared over the last eight years. Their impact upon international competitiveness was, and is still, compensated by periodic adjustments of exchange rates.

A monetary union would effectively equalize national differences in rates of increase of the money supply, and hence provide a powerful push to the equalization of national rates of money inflation. This could help to further reduce existing differences of cost pressures as rational trade union leaders respond to the new macroeconomic environment.

To the extent that this effect should fail to materialize, however, countries with above-average cost increases would necessarily lose market shares and employment. While cost pressures will often respond to changing market conditions, that is not universally so. The increase of nominal unit labour costs in particular (which depends upon the rise of labour productivity and of wages) is strongly influenced by the institutional conditions of national industrial relations systems—both on the shop floor and in collective wage bargaining. There are certain conditions (competition between several independent unions, highly decentralized wage bargaining, and shop floor control over the definition and assignment of jobs) which make it extremely difficult for union leaders to exercise wage restraint and to agree to productivity-increasing changes in work organization and production technology.

As already pointed out above (12.1.5), institutional changes in voluntary organizations like trade unions are difficult to achieve. There have been some instances of industrial relations reform in Europe in recent years (for example, in the legal framework in the United Kingdom, and in shop-floor practices in some leading Italian enterprises). However, there is no general model in sight that might plausibly become the means for any fundamental convergence in different countries' practices. What the Community can provide is a structure within which positive demonstration effects might come to operate in favour of best practices.

The Commission has, in recent years, encouraged the processes of 'social dialogue' at the Community level over questions of labour costs, employment conditions, and economic policy in general. For example, the Community has solicited, and in some degree obtained, the support of employers and trade unions for the Annual Economic Report [37]. Moreover, the Single European Act includes, in Article 118B, the idea that these processes of social dialogue might lead to 'contractual relations' at the European level.

Contrasting with these potential problems of an insufficient capacity to change, it is sometimes argued in the Community that social security regimes and employment protection provisions, indeed wage levels also, risk being excessively depreciated by countries in search of unfair competitive advantages, akin to competitive devaluations of the exchange rate or industrial subsidies. The Community has set up the European Monetary System in part to exclude 'competitive' or 'overshooting' devaluations. Therefore, so the argument may go, there should be analogous constraints on other types of unfair competition. There are important reasons why the first category of variables (pay levels, social security regimes, and employment protection laws) should not be considered analogous to a second category consisting of the exchange rate (or of subsidies of a sector- or firm-specific nature). The first category of variables are extremely unlikely to evolve to the point of overshooting, i.e. to obtain an excessively large competitive improvement. They are only partly instruments of government policy in any case. Moreover, the power of political and interest groups in restraining the erosion of pay, social security, or labour laws is strong. The risk that these variables are manipulated by governments unduly vigorously to obtain unfair competitive advantage is correspondingly slight.

In conclusion, it is vital that countries retain freedom to adjust labour market costs and conditions when exchange rates and subsidies are increasingly constrained by common rules. It is possible, and indeed desirable, that with increasing economic and monetary integration in the areas of industrial relations and wage-bargaining there is a progressive convergence on models that demonstrate positive results. However, this process should not be forced by harmonizing legislation.

12.2.3 *A decentralized model for budgetary and labour policies*

What emerges from this short discussion of macroeconomic policy issues is a decentralized model for budgetary policy and incomes, social policy, and labour regulations.

Consistency in budgetary policies is to be expected more by constraints upon national budget balances and public debt imposed by market conditions, with reduced possibilities for independent monetary financing, than by central directives.

If the co-ordination of macroeconomic policy is to be strengthened more systematically, then the system will need a clearer macroeconomic standard. At times in the past, gold and key currencies have provided such a standard. However, looking ahead to a more developed EMS, a standard with qualities of symmetry will be required as an aid to policy co-ordination. There are different ways of envisaging the workings of such a system. An earlier section (12.1) discussed a number of ideas in the context of the organization of the EMS, and the possible properties of macroeconomic indicators that could serve as standards are discussed in more technical detail in Annex C. However, such standards are unlikely to become automatically binding rules.

Policy towards industrial relations systems, social security, employment protection regulations, and pay determination are also seen as remaining decentralized. Community efforts in the past to legislate in some of these areas with harmonization directives have, in the Group's judgement, not been particularly successful or even functionally necessary. There is a strong case for national experimentation in these policy areas. Equally, there is a strong case for the dissemination of information and exchanges of experience, with a view to positive demonstration effects gradually producing convergence on best practices. But a clearer distinction (in relation to some proposals that emerge in the Community in these areas of policy) needs to be drawn between voluntary convergence on the basis of decentralized choices, and obligatory harmonization on the basis of centralized legislation.

13

The Community Budget and the Redistribution Function

13.1 General considerations

This chapter concerns both the distribution function in Community policies and the Community budget. There is a considerable degree of overlap between the two, which is why they are discussed together. However, not only the budget has distributive consequences. Trade policies do too, for example. And the budget is not wholly devoted to distributive objectives. The Agricultural and Regional Funds, for example, combine allocative and distributive functions. Budget subsidies for research and development are wholly allocative in purpose. These reserves need to be kept in mind.

Since the Community is a political entity whose content is principally of an economic nature, it is inevitably concerned with the broad balance of economic advantages that it offers to its Member States. Elsewhere, the frontiers of economic communities often coincide with the frontiers of defence communities or with the provision and preservation of other 'public goods' such as security, justice, common culture, language, and heritage. In such cases, non-economic values may easily outweigh episodic disadvantages for some regions of an economic nature. The European Community, by contrast, has at present a narrower range of policy functions with which to assure a satisfactory overall balance of advantage for all its Member States. The public good of 'unity' may thus require a relatively greater amount of attention than would be necessary if the Community extended its functions to wider policy areas.

The Community has therefore always needed a redistribution function, and will need it even more in the future given that the spatial distribution of the gains from market integration cannot be relied upon to be an even one (this point is justified further below). The Community's redistribution function can none the less be kept apart from the major national mechanisms of income distribution, such as personal income tax and social security finance.

The Community's concern with distribution issues should basically be limited to where the Community's own policies raise serious issues of equity. This breaks down in practice into three categories:

1. Where the *opening of markets* has an important impact on the spatial distribution (by country or region) of productive activity, and therefore also on spatial income distribution.

2. Where *specific Community policies* have important income distribution

effects without affecting so much the distribution of productive activity, and here agricultural price support is the main example.

3. Where the Community's *own budget* raises conventional issues of fiscal equity, through its financing.

In pursuing the most appropriate design for the distribution function, it is necessary to steer a difficult course between two opposite dangers—the Scylla and Charibdis of Community distribution policy. On the one hand is the danger that Member States may seek to secure a net balance of advantage on each and every Community policy, particularly where there are transparent financial flows at work. Indeed, the economic consequences of Community membership extend far beyond the incidence of its budget. This danger, often referred to as the problem of '*juste retour*', risks undermining the capacity of sectoral policies to achieve their specific objectives, and thence the utility of developing new policy initiatives, and in an extreme situation risks paralysing the Community system as a whole. On the other hand, there is the danger that imbalances in the distribution of the benefits from Community policies may become so serious as to cause mounting political dissatisfaction with the Community in some countries, leading first to non-cooperativeness and ultimately the threat of secession.

To steer a course between the dangers described is a matter for judgement to be formulated in the political process within Member States and Community institutions. As such, it falls outside the competence of this Group. At the economic level, it is not impossible to design instruments that can, when combined with careful political agreements, provide a technical base for a chosen policy. The Community has indeed, in recent years, devoted much time and effort to these matters. In the Group's opinion, this effort has tended to be much more costly politically than might have been the case if the mechanisms of the Community budget were better designed to reconcile efficiency and equity objectives. The principal objective of this chapter is, therefore, to make suggestions to this end.

None the less, it must be stressed that the overall judgement over costs and benefits of participation in the Community must be made in a wider context than merely the budget. Gains from trade are likely for most countries to be of greater significance. Wider still are benefits of a purely political character, such as support for democracy and other political values.

13.2 Redistributive mechanisms in multi-tier government

It is worth recalling the main features of redistributive mechanisms that have been established in multi-tier governmental environments. These were analysed in detail in an earlier report of a Study Group of the Commission [31], chaired by Sir D. MacDougall, and figures quoted in this section are taken from this source. Confederations and federations provide some examples, but countries with national–regional–local governmental structures are also relevant. The examples analysed in the study quoted were all monetary unions in which there is an implicit contract within the union: the freedom to adjust exchange rates is withdrawn, and instead there are budgetary mechanisms for inter-regional or inter-state solidarity. Where the degree of exchange rate fixity is less, it is natural to expect less high-powered mechanisms for budgetary transfers. The budgetary mechanisms of monetary unions therefore offer an extreme point of reference for the Community to bear in mind.

A general pattern emerges in the analysis of confederal, federal and unitary states of a substantial redistribution of resources from rich to poor regions, or from low unemployment to high unemployment regions.

In the MacDougall Report, it was shown that net flows of public finance between the richest and poorest regions of the industrialized monetary unions were generally in the range of 3 to 10 per cent of the product of the receiving region or state. Regions that are small, poor, and geographically peripheral tend to receive even larger net transfers (e.g. 11 per cent of regional product for Brittany, 16 per cent for Northern Ireland, 24 per cent for Calabria). More broadly based calculations showed that in five federations (Germany, Australia, Canada, Switzerland, and the United States), the redistributive impact of federal public finance at the inter-state level reduced per capita income differences by about one-third. For three unitary states (France, Italy, and the United Kingdom), the equivalent figures was a little higher, ranging between a third and a half.

The mechanisms of this redistribution in the five above federations in the early 1970s were on average as shown in Table 13.1. From these figures, it is clear that the two categories of inter-governmental grants were relatively

TABLE 13.1   The redistributive impact of federal public finance

	% redistributive power	% of GDP
Federal taxation and social security receipts	4	15.0
Federal direct public expenditures (defence, social security, etc.)	12	14.5
Specific purpose grants from the federation to the states	7	2.5
General purpose grants from the federation to the states	12	1.2
TOTAL	35	—

Source: MacDougall Report [31].
Note: Based on data for Germany, Australia, Canada, Switzerland, and the US in the early 1970s. The figures will have changed somewhat but not fundamentally in the intervening years.

'Redistributive power' is defined as the (percentage) degree to which inter-state per capita income differences are equalized as a result of inter-state flows of public finance. The '% of GDP' figures indicate the amount of expenditure for each category, for the unweighted average of the five federations.

small in volume terms within the total federal budgets (under 4 per cent of GDP) but high powered in terms of their inter-state redistributive impact, accounting for over half of the total inter-state redistribution. They are also the types of instrument most relevant for the Community budget in the future.

Specific purpose grants (alternatively called 'matching grants') are already prominent in the Community budget in the case of the structural funds (Regional, Social, Agricultural Guidance Section, Integrated Mediterranean Programmes). General-purpose grants feature in the Community budget only in *ad hoc* budgetary settlements in favour of the United Kingdom under the Fontainebleau Agreement.

Specific purpose, matching grants will often combine resource allocation and redistribution objectives. Under such mechanisms the centre may offer a subsidy element, defined perhaps as a contribution of between 25 and 75 per cent of the total subsidy, the remainder being financed at the state or regional level. The centre thus provides an incentive for the state or region to give a higher priority to the policy in question. For the incentive to be effective, it has to operate at the margin of the expenditure programme of the lower government. The centre's fund must be sufficiently open-ended to match an expanded programme of expenditure by the lower government. Otherwise the centre's grant, when effectively defined as a quota of money that cannot match a programme expansion, becomes just a lump-sum grant. A redistribution function may be fulfilled, but the resource allocation function is lost. These principles[1] strongly support the efforts of the Commission to reform the structural funds away from a set of quota allocations, in favour of programme financing that offers real incentives. (This is returned to more specifically below.) The correct way to combine redistribution and resource allocation objectives in a single instrument is through the use of variable matching ratios. Poorer recipients may be offered high matching grants (say 75 per cent). Rich recipients may be offered low matching grants (say 25 per cent), or in the extreme case zero (i.e. ineligible).

The degree of administrative centralization in matching grant programmes can be quite variable, depending upon whether the centre follows a project or programme appraisal method. Under the programme approach, the centre is mainly concerned with evaluation of the policy design of the programme. Once the programme is agreed, all eligible projects are then more or less automatically financed. Only sample investigations are made at the project implementation level. The Community has been tending increasingly towards the programme approach, and the Group judges this to be appropriate.

The principle behind general-purpose equalization mechanisms is that state

---

[1] The microeconomic principles underlying the role of specific-purpose matching grant mechanisms are clearly established in the theory of fiscal federalism [1] and public finance [2].

or local governments are given an equal opportunity to implement public sector programmes to a given standard. Such systems exist in Germany and other federations, including Australia and Canada. The actual mechanisms in these federations vary in many details, but are of the same family. The 'needs' of the states are evaluated, in terms of the cost of given standards of public investments or services. The 'fiscal capacity' of each state is evaluated by calculating what harmonized tax bases would yield to each state. The equalization mechanism then transfers a sum of money reducing, to a given degree, gaps between 'needs' and 'fiscal capacity'. The German equalization system (*Länderfinanzausgleich*) has the particular feature that the final financial settlements are made as direct transfers from rich to poor Länder, raising the poorer Länder to a fiscal capacity of 95 per cent of the federal average. There is no federal control over the actual use of the transfers, since these are general purpose grants.

Specific-purpose matching grant mechanisms are more suitable for the Community as a primary instrument, since they can combine a distributive function with an allocative objective such as regional development. General purpose equalization is more suitable as a primary instrument in mature and homogeneous federations where the uses to which financial transfers are put need not be controlled by the centre. However, general purpose equalization mechanisms have features that are potentially relevant for the Community, such as the quantification of 'needs' and 'fiscal capacity'. They may have a useful residual function in the Community budget, and the Group makes some suggestions in this regard in a later section.

13.3 The regional dimension

Just as capital market liberalization will affect drastically the operating environment for monetary policy in the EMS, so also a triple challenge in the 'real' economy is going to intensify the need for an adequate regional policy in the Community. This triple challenge consists of the internal market programme, the enlargement of the Community, and new trends in industrial technologies. Increased openness of product and factor markets certainly generates economic gains in the aggregate. However, the spatial distribution of such gains is less certain and is unlikely to be even.

Regions tend towards an equalization of incomes per head as a result of the mobility of capital and labour only under severe and unrealistic conditions, such as the absence of economies of scale or of specific locational factors influencing the investment decision [32]. When these and other conditions are not satisfied, the outcome in terms of regional convergence or divergence becomes uncertain. Any easy extrapolation of 'invisible hand' ideas to the real world of regional economics in the presence of market-opening measures would be unwarranted in the light of economic history and theory.

Indeed, other theories draw attention to 'cumulative causation' processes, in which vicious and virtuous cycles of development can emerge in different regions of a single integrated economy [32]. Principal factors in these theories are the economies of scale offered by centrally located urban agglomerations, as well as production economies of scale enjoyed by large enterprises. The production economies of scale also lead in many industries to problems of oligopolistic competition. These factors make it difficult for a backward economic region to catch up on the performance of leading economic regions.

Within the *internal market* programme, there may be other elements likely to be helpful to backward or declining regions, and some that are likely to work in a contrary direction. Improvements in the competitiveness of transport and telecommunication services should, for example, reduce the locational disadvantage of peripheral regions. On the other hand, the liberalization of financial services seems likely to emphasize the economies of scale offered by specialized centres. This is illustrated rather clearly in current developments in the City of London, which is gaining market share in relation to other British and European financial centres. The liberalization of government procurement would work both ways. It would cause a considerable rationalization of activities, such as in the production of railway and energy-generating equipment in traditional industrial centres. The previously highly protected producers of such equipment are going to be subject to enormous adaptations. On the other hand, the terms of trade would be improved for buyers of such equipment, and this will be particularly beneficial for the smaller, peripheral countries.

The sharpest regional challenges are likely to emerge as a result of the combination of *enlargement* and internal market opening. This is because the Community's latest enlargements have substantially widened the range of productivity differences between the core industrial areas and the least developed regions. For example, the ratio of Ireland's income per capita to that of Denmark is 1 to 1.8 (in purchasing power parity terms); the ratio of Portugal to Denmark is 1 to 2.8. As is explained in Annex A, this wider range of income per capita levels means also that the nature of the market integration process will tend to be qualitatively different. Between economies of similar economic structures and levels of development, trade integration proceeds with expanded *intra*-industry trade, which is relatively favourable to a smooth adjustment of the industrial structure to more competitive conditions. Between much more different economies, trade integration is more likely to be based on expanded *inter*-industry trade, in which the exploitation of opportunities for comparative advantage may involve a more radical shake-out of entire industries and much intenser specializations in industrial structure by region. In this case, the adjustment processes may be relatively severe, warranting active intervention by the public authorities.

In addition, current trends in industrial structure in favour of *high technology* industries mean on the whole an aggravation of the problems of, especially, backward and peripheral regions, and sometimes the old, declining industrial regions. There are strong tendencies for high technology industries (such as electronics and informatics) to cluster together, mostly in areas characterized by excellent transport locations and telecommunications facilities, an abundant supply of highly skilled labour, the proximity of major academic and research centres, and the proximity also of major financial centres. These industries also show a certain aversion to older industrial centres, at least those with physically less attractive environments. In the United Kingdom, this is contributing to an increasingly deep north–south divide in economic fortunes, with a similar (albeit globally less problematic) trend in Germany. Industrial and technology policies in the Community are strongly directed towards improving the Community's competitiveness in these industries. Success in these policies could represent a strategic economic advance for the Community, but it could also aggravate the problem of regional disparities unless explicit action is taken to reduce the locational handicaps of presently least-favoured regions.

The problems of structural change in industry may be particularly acute for some of the old industrial areas of lower-income Member States. Comparative advantage in some of the medium-technology industries presently suffering from crises of overcapacity (steel, ship-building, etc.) may lie in these economies, contrasting with the comparative advantage in high technology of the highest-income countries, and the comparative advantage in simple manufacturing in third world countries. If quota regimes or capacity restraints in crisis sectors in the Community were to block the growth of market shares of such countries or regions having a comparative advantage, then the risks of divergent regional trends would be accentuated. In this respect, a truly free internal market would be the best policy for the regions with low labour costs (this confirms the argument in 11.1). The removal of market distortions of these kinds is clearly a more efficient policy than one of increasing subsidies from the structural funds to compensate for the market distortions.

Finally, there is the question how these issues are affected by the aggregate rate of economic *growth* in the Community. There are both theoretical and empirical grounds for considering that high levels of economic activity are helpful to the least favoured regions. As demand pressures rise in an economy, skilled labour resources in the most-favoured regions become fully used. Congestion and rising property prices add to the incentives for giving more attention to the least-favoured regions as investment locations. Conversely, in periods of weak demand pressure, the least-favoured regions would tend to be hit hardest. Something like this appears to have been happening in the Community in the two periods before and after the 1973 breakpoint. (Annex E provides information on actual regional divergences in the Community, and past trends.) In the earlier period of high growth and low unemployment, regional inequalities of income per capita—both at the intra-country and inter-country levels—were declining. In the subsequent period, these trends have been reversed. In the last ten years of sharply rising aggregate unemployment, the disparities between unemployment rates have also risen sharply (also at both intra- and inter-country levels). We shall return to this problem in Chapter 14.

The Single European Act therefore rightly suggests, in Article 130A to E, a wide conception of how the Community should assure its 'economic and social cohesion'. The structural funds, to which the next section is devoted, is certainly of crucial importance. However, there are several other branches of policy which will also be important in this context. The conditions of macroeconomic growth in the Community as a whole has been mentioned. Of equal if not greater importance is the need for macro- and microeconomic policies in the countries with the weakest regions to be coherent with the market-opening strategy of the Community. In addition, there are several further categories of Community policy that should contribute to the 'cohesion' objective. These include policy towards state subsidies (rich regions should not be permitted to out-compete poorer regions in this respect); policy towards industrial R&D (attention has to be given to avoiding a bias in favour of the most developed regions); and the avoidance of quota regimes that prevent weaker regions from exploiting their comparative advantages (as argued above). Overall, therefore, the Community has a considerable range of instruments with which to work for 'cohesion' across its regions. These will be needed.

13.4 Reform of the structural funds

The Group favours the rationalization of the existing structural funds under a simplified, coherent body of regulations that would embrace and reshape the present Regional Fund, the Social Fund, the Agricultural Guidance Fund, and the Integrated Mediterranean Programmes without merging them from an administrative point of view. The structural funds would thus share common features favouring their coherent application in problem areas and facilitating the articulation of Community priorities.

The structural funds would support the major categories of capital formation required to endow the regions with a strong productive potential:

Human capital
— as a first priority, aid to vocational training and retraining, and technical assistance
— in second place, and in the case of only the poorest regions or countries, financial support for general education

Physical capital
— aid to investment, with a strong emphasis on appropriate economic infrastructure

Budgetary grants from the structural funds would firstly finance human

capital formation and physical infrastructural investment. For private production investment, the Community's lending instruments should play a more
important role, with budgetary grants for the co-financing of national
investment incentives as a complementary aid. (Links between budgetary
subsidies and loan finance are discussed explicitly later in this section.)

The support for general education in the poorest areas would be an
innovation. Two arguments favour this. First, it would correspond to these
areas' priority needs, which are indeed very different to those that stimulated
the Community's first social policy activities (e.g. retraining steel and coal
workers). Second, there is the problem that countries like Portugal and
Ireland, actually or potentially, see a significant proportion of their public
expenditure on education flow abroad through emigration. This is a striking
example of the external 'leakage' of public expenditure benefits that may
warrant subsidy from the centre. It is in the interest neither of the region of
emigration nor of immigration that the region of emigration reduce its
investment in education under the burden of these 'leakages'.

For each category of capital formation *ceiling levels* of expenditure would be
set at a level relating to the needs of the regions, which might be assessed in
relation to but not necessarily equal to the Community average. (Some
background data in this regard have been assembled in Annex E.) The Funds
would then offer the incentive of matching grants, variable as a function of
relative income levels of countries, for suitable programmes of expenditure up
to these ceiling levels. The Community subsidy would thus (in accordance
with the principles described in 13.2 above) cheapen for the public authority
of the recipient region the tax price of the development programmes in
question, and therefore help assure additional total expenditure on this
function. The Community would in this way help achieve a reallocation of
resources within the recipient economy as well as transfer resources. 'Additionality' would be achieved in a decentralized manner through the working
of incentive mechanisms, not by a centralized attempt by the Community to
negotiate 'additionality' in relation to the budgetary projections of Member
States. The ceiling levels would clearly *not* represent automatic rights; indeed,
they might most often not be reached, the volume of Community expenditure
being limited rather by quality control mechanisms (see further below).

Incentive mechanisms of this type contrast with quota allocations of funds.
Experience shows, in the Community as in other multi-tier governmental
settings, that quota allocations of subsidies prove invariably to be fungible with
other uses, so undermining the intended additionality impact on the expenditure category in question. One of the purposes of rationalizing the Funds should
be to eliminate these kinds of design defects in existing regulations. This
supports partial reforms that have been made for example in the Regional Fund
regulation in 1984 and in the Integrated Mediterranean Programmes.

It is not the Group's task to make precise proposals on which particular
regions should be eligible for aid from the Funds. At the level of general

principles, we consider the two categories—less developed regions and those suffering from industrial decline—to be plausible.

In terms of objective criteria for less developed regions, one could proceed from the poorest region in terms of income per capita up the hierarchy of regions until 20 per cent of the population were covered. As regards the regions suffering industrial decline, the inclusion of regions covering a further 10 per cent of the population might be plausible. For this second category, the eligibility criteria could begin with the double test of having a relatively low income per capita and a relatively high unemployment rate. The standard here could be around the Community average. Since both criteria would have to be met, far less than half the Community would be eligible, but finer appreciation of regional situations, with the addition of further specific criteria, would no doubt be warranted in drawing up actual operating rules in line with specific development requirements. The main point is that the map of regions eligible for Community funds should increasingly reflect the Community's regional priorities, rather than those of individual countries in the purely national context. For example, it may be appropriate for the Community to aid more regions in Spain than the national authorities have so far been able to afford (proposals along these lines are currently being considered), and less regions in Germany than the public authorities there support. (A detailed listing of the regions of the Community, with income per capita and unemployment levels, is given in Annex E.)

For *industrial areas in decline*, it is important that the Community should be able to come quickly to the aid of a region hit by adverse economic circumstances. The eligibility criteria for such regions should be flexible enough to assure this. It should be clearly understood in public opinion that, while the market-opening process had its risks, the Community was ready to come to the help of a region that found itself with a heavy concentration of adjustment problems. The fortunes of the old industrial regions are likely to be more sensitive to changing conditions of competitiveness in the internal market than the less favoured regions. For the declining industrial regions, it should be expected that they can both enter and leave the list of eligible areas more rapidly than in the case of the backward areas.

A Communication recently addressed by the Commission to the other Community institutions [22] has given considerable attention to the reform of the structural funds. This report was produced in response to the call in the Single European Act (Art. 130A to E concerning 'economic and social cohesion') for a comprehensive proposal for the amendment of the existing funds (Regional, Social, Agricultural Guidance Section).

The Commission's report advocates concentration of the structural funds on five target problems:

1. Backward regions.
2. Declining industrial regions.

3. Long-term unemployment.
4. Employment of young people.
5. Agricultural and rural development.

The Community should indeed be concerned with its less developed regions and those industrial regions adversely affected by major structural changes in supply and demand conditions. However, the Group judges that the Community's direct contribution to easing the problem of unemployment should also be mainly approached in relation to the problems of these two categories of regions, rather than added as further lines of priority action for the whole of the Community's area. As the Community's resources are not sufficient for comprehensive actions to combat labour market and regional imbalances in the whole of the Community's territory, they should be concentrated more selectively on priority problems for which the Community has relatively direct responsibilities. The attempt to reconcile this problem of supply and demand for resources by limiting the labour market actions to narrow criteria (long-term unemployed, youth unemployed) would lead to distortions in labour market policies. The Group has heard reports in several countries on how these criteria are difficult to match with the priority labour market programmes of national authorities, especially in the less-developed Community countries. In these countries, there are priority needs for basic education and vocational training, including capital investment in teaching institutions and in teacher-training facilities. The present operating criteria of the Social Fund need to be reconsidered in this light.

The Guidance section of the Agricultural Fund should intensify its redirection of resources away from raising productivity for commodities in surplus, and towards redeploying land use into activities which are either non-agricultural (tourism, recreational uses, etc.) or producing commodities that are not in surplus (forestry, organic products, etc.).

The Commission has, in its recent Communications to the Council and European Parliament [22, 35], proposed raising the present level of expenditures under the structural funds from the 1987 level of 7 billion ECUs of commitments to 14 billion ECUs in 1992 (at constant prices). The latter figure would, for example, represent transfers of about 2 per cent of the present GDP, or 10 per cent of the present gross capital formation of the poorest regions covering 30 per cent of the Community's population. Such a sum would be sufficient for making a matching contribution to the raising of capital formation in the weaker regions to levels consistent with a progressive reduction in regional disparities. However, as a share of the Community's total GDP (0.3 per cent), this sum is under one-tenth of the volume of intergovernmental grants observed in the federations of the industrialized world (i.e. federation-to-state grants, as reported in 13.2 above).

The structural funds would operate in co-ordination with the *lending instruments* for which the borrowing is undertaken by the Commission[2] and, principally, the European Investment Bank (EIB), the Community's long-term credit institution, whose role has been underlined by the provisions introduced into the Treaty by the Single European Act. The volume and scope of EIB lending has consistently grown over the years (+21% per annum over the period 1970–86 in ECUs), alongside the progressive establishment of common policies. Its main area of intervention is the financing of investments, from small to very large ventures, promoted by private and public initiative, in all sectors of the economy—industry, agriculture and services, energy, economic infrastructure. The EIB priority objective is the development of the less-favoured regions of the Community. The EIB also operates toward the attainment of the Community energy objectives, the improvement of communications between Member Countries, protection of the environment, the modernization or conversion of productive capacity, and the competitiveness of Community industry. Total lending for investment purposes by Community institutions amounted to about 8.7 billion ECUs in 1986, of which 6.7 was from EIB own resources and 0.4 billion from NCI.

With the liberalization of capital markets, shortages of savings in the less developed regions and countries is likely to cease to be a constraint on their economic development. The effective constraint will be the rate of return to capital. The Community's loan-financing instruments can help develop the workings of local capital markets and credit institutions, for example through the provision of global loans for on-lending to small and medium-sized enterprises. However, where the rate of return is insufficient to attract finance on commercial terms, the provision of interest rate subsidies from the structural funds may be required to help boost investment and the use of Community loan instruments. These subsidies may be justified by the need to overcome locational disadvantages and offset the agglomeration economies of scale enjoyed by central areas. The possibility for the Regional Fund to provide subsidies in this way already exists (in the Fund's Regulation), but has not in practice been exploited. Consideration should therefore be given to organizing expanded co-operation in the operations of the structural funds and the loan instruments. In this way, increased flows of private capital into the less-developed regions could be actively induced alongside the expansion of the structural funds.

As regards *quality control* over the use of funds, the Group supports the Commission's move in favour of a programme-funding approach as the basic method. The Community institutions should not become involved in the detail of project evaluation, except in the case of very large projects, or where clear issues of Community interest arise (or where the European Investment

---

[2] The Commission's borrowing and lending instruments operate under three powers: the European Coal and Steel Community (ECSC); the New Community Instrument (NCI); and Euratom. The NCI and Euratom lending functions are managed through the agency of the European Investment Bank.

Bank and other loan instruments are concerned with 'bankable' projects). The Commission should, however, be empowered to investigate ex-post the quality of programmes that the Funds finance, and to have powers to suspend financing of programmes that are found to be poorly managed.

These evaluations might best be conducted by a specialized inspection service of the Commission, which would be apart from the departments responsible for the policy of the funds. This inspectorate would thus undertake audits, in the field as well as in Brussels, of all the structural funds, and so be able to report in an objective way on the quality of local programme management as well as the coherence of the operating criteria of the Funds set at the Community level. The policies guiding management of the existing Funds are currently reviewed by a number of official committees, including representatives of the Commission and Member States (the Regional Policy Committee is an example). As a complement to present efforts to improve the overall coherence of the Funds, a responsibility for overall policy review could be assigned to the Economic Policy Committee.

In the event that the structural funds were substantially increased, and the eligibility criteria broadened to relatively wide programme categories, consideration could be given to associating the Funds in some circumstances with *macroeconomic policy conditions*. There is a gap in the present set of Community instruments in the following sense. The balance of payments loan mechanism, used in the past by Greece, France, Italy, and Ireland, associates macroeconomic policy conditions for a relatively short period (two to three years) with loans. The structural funds at present supply grants according to purely microeconomic criteria. A new, combined formula could be one in which a 'super-tranche' of grants from the structural funds might be agreed alongside a medium-term programme (of up to five years) to achieve and consolidate stability and support a macroeconomic strategy which incorporates structural policies and reforms. Several of the poorest Member States have public sector deficits of the order of 10 per cent of GDP or more which have a considerable structural component. These deficits need urgently to be set on a medium-term trajectory for reduction to sustainable levels. It would be hard to justify the Community extending much increased budgetary assistance to these countries unless their macroeconomic strategies were simultaneously directed towards financial stability in the medium-term. More precisely, such macroeconomic conditionality could be operative where the total of budgetary receipts of a low-income country exceeded the bands of the safeguard mechanism described below (in section 13.7).

To summarize, the reform of the structural funds should, in the Group's judgement, have the following features:

1. A simpler set of priorities, such as to support the strengthening or recovery of productive potential in the less-developed and industrially declining regions; with coherence in the body of implementing regulations,

relating to regional maps of eligibility and Community financial participation rates; and a substantial expansion in their total volume.

2. An emphasis on programme rather than project financing, with wider and more flexible eligibility criteria, decentralized incentive features in the design of funds, and avoidance of rigid quota allocations.

3. Creation of a quality-control inspectorate, and possible links between the availability of 'super-tranches' from the structural funds and medium-term macroeconomic strategies.

4. Greater association of the structural funds with the operations of the European Investment Bank and New Community Instrument, with subsidies from the former to aid expansion of the latter.

13.5 The mix of allocation and distribution in agricultural policy

The Group has not investigated the vast and complex area of Common Agricultural Policy and its reform. A brief reference is made in the present chapter for two reasons. First, the Common Agricultural Policy has evolved to the point that its income distributive effects have become a dominant aspect. Secondly, there is no chance for a profound restructuring of the Community budget that does not include regaining effective control over agricultural spending.

The Common Agricultural Policy was given at the outset multiple objectives—security of supplies, steady incomes for farmers, fair prices for consumer. But it was given basically only one instrument, price support. In its objective to assure a high degree of self-sufficiency the policy has proved all too successful. Structural and income aid instruments were also created but have remained of small importance. The income objective was largely satisfied, but at prices that were or became relatively high and which created a structural divergence between production increases of the order of 3 per cent a year, and demand increases of under 0.5 per cent. The Community's problem has been aggravated by the emergence of excess supply in world food markets, due also to the green revolution in the third world. The situation was quite unforeseen ten to fifteen years ago. Over time, the ratio of direct or indirect subsidies to value added has risen in the Community to the point that they now account for well over half of the net income of the sector. The balance between the allocation function and the distribution function has shifted massively in favour of the distribution function.

This represents a systemic anomaly, since the Community is in principle well suited to executing allocative, market policies, but it is not well suited to executing distributive policies at the level of individual persons and small enterprises. Efficient income distribution policies require detailed administration at the level of the individual, and coherence with features of income tax and social security systems, and the Community cannot assure this. The Community has thus switched roles with the Member States, counter to the basic principles of subsidiarity and comparative advantage. Indeed, the Community's agricultural policy mechanisms have also become an increasingly inefficient technique of income distribution policy as such. In its effort now to limit production, recourse has been made to quotas in the milk sector. This deepens the Community's responsibility for income distribution, since it is now presiding over systems for the award of fixed economic rents to individual farm owners; by the same token, the Community withdraws even further from efficient resource allocation policy.

The Group therefore approves of the principles set out in the Commission's 1985 Green Paper on agricultural policy [33] and its recent Communication to the Council [22] which advocate a reorientation of policy back towards using the price instrument for medium-term market balance objectives, with greater reliance on income maintenance for social policy purposes.

However, current actions (reductions in milk quotas, some relaxation of support price guarantees) represent only limited progress in this direction. Moreover, the Council of Ministers is still exerting pressure for support prices higher than the levels proposed by the Commission. Support prices should tend towards world price levels (although the significance of world prices for efficient resource allocation differs according to products).

The Council's role in fixing farm prices is related to a particular feature of the Council's decision-making structure, notably that each sectoral formation of the Council has equal legislative power. The Group believes that institutional changes should be made to correct the adverse effects that this has on budgetary control.[3] One proposal made recently [34], would have the Agricultural Fund separated from the general budget. The point of so doing would be to allow Finance Ministers to decide the annual budgetary ceiling of the Agricultural Fund, with Farm Ministers retaining responsibility for the specifics of agricultural policy and for adjustments required to respect the budgetary ceiling. Thus there would be no automatic spill-over of unbudgeted expenditure requirements to the passing of supplementary budgets, or reduction in non-agricultural expenditures. Since agricultural expenditures are determined automatically by the evolution of production and world prices, changes would have to be made in the mechanisms of policy to avoid expenditure overruns. While Finance Ministers might be able to agree upon a medium-term programme to control firmly the present level of farm spending, other institutional innovations might be needed to secure a durable change of policy. In fact, changes in this direction are now being made as the open-ended guarantees are being curtailed with production ceilings and with the

[3] For the European Parliament to have some power of co-decision over the Agricultural Fund, it would be necessary to abolish or modify the present distinction between 'obligatory' expenditure (largely agricultural) and 'non-obligatory' expenditure (other expenditures). The Parliament has no power over the final determination of obligatory expenditures, but has a limited margin of power over non-obligatory expenditures. This margin is determined in relation to the so-called 'maximum rate' of increase for the budget, which is a function of certain macroeconomic aggregates. This system is explained in detail elsewhere [21].

possibility to suspend the intervention price guarantee in some degree for some products. Indeed, consideration should be given to mechanisms that would trigger *automatic* adjustments to market support policies when budgetary over-runs emerge; thus there should be no requirement for further decisions by the Council to implement such changes.

A medium-term programme to reduce Community spending on agriculture would of course have repercussions on farm incomes. In such a case, the Community should work out a new set of rules to determine what types of national farm income support were acceptable or unacceptable from the point of view of the Community. A strong preference should be given to aids that were *ad personam* for present farmers until their retirement. Quota systems of the type introduced for milk products should also only operate *ad personam* for present farmers. Over half the Community's farming population is 55 years old or more. The Community should let this demographic factor work positively for agricultural market adjustment.

Major adjustments of agricultural policy of the type envisaged should be implemented gradually over a medium-term period, not abruptly. The present structure of farm incomes results in large measure from past policy decisions, so policy changes have to give time to adjust and alternative opportunities to those most affected.

Concern is often expressed, understandably, about ideas for 're-nationalizing' agricultural policy. The Group advocates (a) 're-Communitarising' the allocation function through unifying farm prices at a lower level and abolishing internal border tariffs and subsidies, and (b) decentralizing a larger part of the distribution function at present done at a Community level, subject to Community constraints to avoid disguised production subsidies.

13.6 Financing of the Community budget and its overall equity

In the last ten years, the Community has spent enormous political resources —in terms of both the time of ministers and its own public credibility—over budget burden-sharing issues. It risks doing so again, with the prospective phasing out of the transitional arrangements for the new Member States and the imminent exhaustion of the increase in own resources agreed in 1984.

Accordingly, it is important to devise budgetary arrangements which minimize distributive conflict and embody so far as possible incentives for sound policy-making.

As regards the financing of the budget, the first own resources are (and should remain) customs duties and agricultural levies. The marginal source is at present levied on the basis of the value-added tax. From an equity point of view, this key is not without problems, because it is biased against countries which have a low share of investment in GDP, and in favour of countries which have poor collection systems. However, the principle of moving the financing of the Community onto an 'own resource' basis was of great institutional importance, and the Group would not favour any backward step in this respect. The essential element of an 'own resource' is that it accrues to the Community budget automatically, without depending upon any year-by-year decisions to be taken by national budgetary authorities. The Group has not studied the question of how best the Community's own resource system should develop. The Commission has proposed [35] a new marginal key based on GNP to supplement the existing value-added tax revenues, which would introduce a clear standard of distributive neutrality with respect to national income levels. Without taking a position, therefore, on the exact form of the Community's next own resources, the Group does make the point that budgetary reforms should *inter alia* be designed to ensure to the highest possible degree an automatically equitable Community budget. The marginal financing source could, accordingly, be given a profile of some fiscal progressivity. Some illustrative formulae for this are presented in Annex D. The basic principle would be the same as that employed in most personal income taxes. The tax rate rises as a percentage of income, as the per capita income level increases. This is normally justified on the grounds that some progressivity of this kind is required for there to be an 'equality of sacrifice' as between taxable persons of different income levels [2]. Progressivity on the revenue side of the Community budget would alleviate in some degree the need for the expenditure functions of the budget to mix allocative and distributive characteristics.

The various ideas so far discussed for restructuring the Community budget are summarized in a highly schematic way in Panel 13.1, which focuses on three variables: (*a*) the agricultural budget, which might remain constant in GDP share, in volume, or in nominal terms; (*b*) the structural funds and other policies, such as support for R&D, which might then grow either only a little or substantially, given a budget total constrained to a constant GDP share; and (*c*) the marginal financing source, which might be neutral with respect to GNP per capita, or be fiscally progressive. Overall this gives rise to six scenarios.

The Group's preference would be for a restructuring of the Community budget that went in the direction of increasing the structural funds substantially in real terms, and decreasing the share of agricultural spending in a budget whose total size should not grow faster than GNP. Thus scenario 3, or scenario 6 in the event of a progressive marginal financing source, would be favoured. The Group would recommend a significant expansion of the budget total only with adequate measures to control agricultural expenditure. However, the most restrictive scenario for Community agricultural expenditure could be associated with some expansion of national expenditures on income support for farmers.

In the event that the budget evolved in this direction, the equity issues of burden-sharing could to a larger degree than in the past be settled automatically. In the enlarged Community of Twelve, these considerations are even more important than they would have been for the Community of nine or ten countries. The particular problem of the United Kingdom has in the past

PANEL 13.1   Illustrative scenarios for the restructuring of the Community
Budget until 1992 (billions of ECU in 1992 prices)

| | Scenarios 1 & 4 | | Scenarios 2 & 5 | | Scenarios 3 & 6 | |
	bn ECU	%	bn ECU	%	bn ECU	%
Agriculture	32	60	27	51	24	45
Structural funds	10	20	14	24	16	29
Other policies	5	7	6	12	7	13
Other expenditure	7	13	7	13	7	13
TOTAL	54	100	54	100	54	100

In these scenarios it is assumed that the budget total is constrained to a GNP
share of 1.1 per cent. Assuming a growth rate of nominal GNP of 6 per cent
per annum (with output growth of 3.5 per cent and prices of 2.5 per cent, the
budget total thus reaches 54 billion ECUs in 1992.

Assumptions made for *agricultural expenditure* are:

Scenario 1: constant in share of GNP.

Scenario 2: constant in real terms.

Scenario 3: constant in nominal (ECU) terms.

Expenditure on the *structural funds* and certain *other policies* (internal
policies, such as R&D etc.) are the residual amount, given also that the sum
'*other expenditure*' (administration, external policies, and miscellaneous) are
held constant in real terms.

The *marginal financing source* in scenarios 1, 2, and 3 is *neutral* with respect to
GNP. Three more *scenarios (4, 5, and 6)* are set out in Annex D, in which a
progressive marginal financing source is assumed, keeping the other variables
as in scenarios 1, 2, and 3. Annex D also illustrates the distributive
implications of the scenarios.

The scenarios, it is stressed, are deliberately simplified and schematic.
Their main purpose is to show the possible scope for restructuring the budget
under a reasonably constrained budget total, and depending upon different
assumptions for agricultural spending.

been settled in an *ad hoc* manner.[4] This practice will become increasingly
problematic as the new Member States approach the end of their transitional
periods, which presently limit their budgetary contributions. The need for the

[4] Shortly before agreement in 1984 of the Fontainebleau Mechanism, which provided *ad hoc*
compensation in the Community budget in favour of the United Kingdom, there were extensive
negotiations over more systematic formulae to correct excessive budgetary imbalances [38, 39].
The Fontainebleau mechanism provided for the United Kingdom to receive a budget rebate
based on two-thirds of the difference between its percentage share in budget expenditures and its
percentage share in VAT contributions. The Commission's proposals in February 1987 for the
future financing of the budget [22] include replacement of the Fontainebleau mechanism by a
formula which would reimburse the United Kingdom for half of the difference between its
percentage share in agricultural expenditure and its percentage share in Community GNP.

years ahead is a set of budget functions that automatically and universally resolves emerging problems of budgetary equity.

To this end, a *safeguard mechanism* of fairly application is set out in Annex D. Its purpose would be to correct inequitable situations arising from the budget. The essence of the mechanism is portrayed graphically in Fig. 13.1. Subject to certain exclusions for budgetary items that cannot be attributed to individual countries, net balances of budgetary expenditures and receipts would be calculated by country. The normative principle would be for these net balances to be progressively (and of course inversely) related to national income per capita. Around a central curve representing this relationship there would be bands that would represent the edges of the safeguard mechanism. Where the budget resulted in countries' situations falling outside these bands, there would be corrective payments to or from the budget until the country's

FIG. 13.1 An equity safeguard mechanism for the Community budget

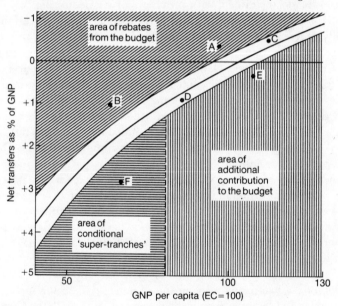

Note: Where the budget led to a result falling outside the bands, there would be a correction to bring the outlying countries back to the edge of the bands. Within the bands, individual Community policies would freely determine the outcome without giving rise to corrective transactions. For countries with low income per capita there would be the possibility for net transfers to exceed the bottom band, depending upon macroeconomic policy conditions (see text). The following are (fictitious) examples:

1. Countries A and B would receive rebates from the budget.
2. Countries C and D would not be directly affected.
3. Country E would make an additional contribution to the budget.
4. Country F would receive 'super-tranches' from the structural funds depending upon macroeconomic conditions.

situation was brought back to the edge of the bands. In the area within the bands, the individual policy functions of the budget would freely determine the net balance outcomes.

A useful distinction could well be made between the cases of budget outcomes falling *above* the bands (the 'unacceptable situations' of excessively onerous budgetary conditions) and outcomes falling *below* the bands. While the 'unacceptable situations' would give rise to a simple rebate to the country concerned, the case of 'excessively generous' budgetary transfers could be treated differently. Where, in this latter case, the country concerned was among the poorest Member States, the possibility of conditional 'super-tranches' to the structural funds (described in 13.4) could be brought into play. Thus, such a country could benefit from budget outcomes more favourable than the normal limit of the safeguard mechanism, *on condition* that agreement was reached with the Community over a medium-term macroeco-nomic and financial strategy, with provision for its monitoring.

The shape of the curve and the width of the bands are both variables that could only be fixed as a result of a political judgement arrived at in the process of Community negotiation. It is not for the Group to recommend specific values. Criteria relevant in choosing the broad shape of the curve are the relative size of poor and rich countries and implicit judgements over the marginal utility of income. Determining the width of the band would in practice depend upon a more complex set of criteria. Details are set out technically in Annex D, including some quantified simulations of the scenarios presented in Panel 13.1. It is not, however, appropriate for the Group to propose particular solutions. The essential objective in introducing a safe-guard mechanism of this type would be to separate out the processes of shaping individual Community policies from concern over their income distribution consequences. In this way, a country's representatives could concentrate on the most desirable policy for agriculture, regional develop-ment, and so on, in its own right. Policies for efficient resource allocation would thus be separated to a higher degree from equity questions. Both efficiency and equity objectives are of essential importance. Insufficient separation of the two in the mechanisms of policy risks seeing unsatisfactory outcomes on both accounts. Such is the present situation with the Community budget, which therefore calls for reform.

14
Growth Conditions

Departing from the institutional and systemic issues discussed in the last three chapters, we now turn briefly to some aspects of macroeconomic policy for the period from now to about 1992, when the internal market is due to be completed. We do so because we regard a satisfactory growth rate as an indispensable condition for the success of the Community's general strategy. The question is whether this satisfactory growth rate will come spontaneously or require special policy initiatives.

The market opening process, by improving the efficiency of resource allocation, will permit a *step up in the level of productivity and output in the economy*. Implemented over a medium-term period, this translates into an increase in the annual potential growth rate for a number of years. In principle, this increase in productivity and output is to be distinguished from the medium-term increase in growth that is required in order to reduce unemployment: this is because the integration of the internal market will in the first instance raise productivity rather than employment. However, the two processes will in all likelihood have to run concurrently. Evidence of a trend reduction in unemployment is likely to be a political condition of a speedy implementation of the internal market programme.

The economic channels whereby *market liberalization* should lead to faster economic growth are well established. With the elimination of trading barriers, competition is increased and prices fall towards the level of the most efficient producers. Prices are further reduced over a period of years as production is rationalized and economies of scale exploited in new investments. The lower prices lead to higher real disposable incomes. Wage inflationary pressures are dampened doubly, directly through the lower prices and indirectly through the sharper competitive pressures bearing upon enterprises. Macroeconomic policies may in principle remain geared to a steady evolution of monetary and national income aggregates. In this case, the lower price rise will leave more room for real economic growth within a framework of a steady evolution of nominal demand. For example, the normative growth component implicit in a money supply growth target could be increased.

As regards policies to reduce *unemployment*, the Community has made some progress in recent years, at least in moving towards a consensus view on the principles of a common strategy. Actual unemployment, of course, has not yet been reduced from its peak level of about 11 per cent in the Community as a whole. The Community has, however, agreed in principle on a 'co-operative growth strategy', as set out in its last two Annual Economic Reports [36, 37], which envisage raising the annual growth rate from its recent trend rate of 2.5 per cent to 3.5 per cent for the period until 1990. (By comparison, growth in the 1960s averaged 4.8 per cent in the Community as a whole). In these conditions, unemployment could be reduced to about 7 per cent by the end of the period. It remains difficult to diagnose at all surely the split of total unemployment between that due to excessively high labour costs and that due to insufficient marcoeconomic demand (the so-called 'classical' and 'Keynesian' components). However, the Community strategy envisages proceeding on both fronts at the same time, with wage moderation alongside macroeconomic policy actions (interest rate reductions, tax reforms, increases in public investment) sustained over a medium-term period. The relative dosage of policies affecting labour costs and macroeconomic demand could be adjusted progressively in the light of results.

The increase in productivity and output obtainable through the internal market programme should thus be seen as supplementary to the acceleration of growth that is made both desirable and possible by the present level of unemployment. If one retains the 3.5 per cent growth rate of the Community macroeconomic strategy, the internal market programme could perhaps raise this for a period of years by up to a further 0.5 per cent per annum,[1] implying, conceivably, an overall growth rate of 4 per cent. Such an outcome would transform the economic environment within the Community. It could only happen as a result of determined supply-side measures in all product and factor markets, domestically and/or at the Community level, with support from suitably expansionary macroeconomic policies.

While the principles of the 'co-operative growth strategy' are entirely reasonable, and growth could further be boosted with vigorous implementation of the internal market programme, it is evident that the desired acceleration of growth is not yet taking place. On the contrary, recent forecasts point to a downward revision of growth prospects for 1987 to below 2.5 per cent.

Failure to secure a robust strengthening of the Community's growth rate would not only mean no reduction in unemployment: it would also seriously undermine politically the chances of implementing the internal market programme and of making a successful integration of the new Member States into the Community economy. The countries of the periphery of the Community should be able to look ahead to a period of rapid growth, as they raise productivity levels closer towards average European standards. The Community's structural funds can help induce the necessary expansion of their investment efforts. The countries of the centre of the Community for

---

[1] This figure is within the range of magnitudes for the growth-enhancing impact of trade liberalization measures noted in 5.1.

their part would profit from this rapidly opening and expanding market. However, this complex process of co-operative interaction has little chance of materializing if the Community's macroeconomic growth rate is not substantially increased during the next critical years when many market-opening measures are due to be taken.

References

[1] Commission of the EC, *Completing the Internal Market: White Paper from the Commission to the European Council.* Luxemburg, 1985.

[2] W. Oates, *Fiscal Federalism.* New York, 1972.

[3] R. and P. Musgrave, *Public Finance in Theory and Practice.* New York, 1973.

[4] W. Gerloff, *Die Deutsche Zoll- und Handelspolitik von der Gründung des Zollvereins bis zum Frieden von Versailles.* Leipzig, 1920.

[5] A Bolino, *The Development of the American Economy.* Columbus, 1966.

[6] R. Bartel, 'International Monetary Unions: The 19th-century experience', *Journal of European Economic History*, 33 (1974).

[7] R. Hawtrey, *The Gold Standard in Theory and Practice.* London, 1947.

[8] A. Sommariva and G. Tullio, *German Macroeconomic History 1880–1979.* London, 1987.

[9] M. Bordo and A. Schwartz, *A Retrospective on the Classical Gold Standard.* New York, 1984.

[10] T. Padoa-Schioppa, *Money, Economic Policy, and Europe*, European Perspectives. Commission of the EC, Brussels, 1985.

[11] N. Owen, *Economies of Scale, Competitiveness, and Trade Patterns within the European Community.* Oxford, 1983.

[12] A. Jacquemin and A. Sapir, *Intra-EC Trade: A Sectoral Analysis.* Centre for European Policy Studies, Brussels, 1986.

[13] P. Buigues and P. Goybet, *The Competitivity of European Industry*, European Economy no. 25, Commission of the EC, Brussels, 1986.

[14] B. Heitgen, *Import Protection and Economic Performance: Their Impact on Economic Growth*, Kiel Institute of World Economics, 1986.

[15] H. Giersch, *Internal and External Liberalisation for Faster Growth.* Economic Papers, Commission of the EC, 1987.

[16] J. Pelkmans and Vollebergh, 'The Traditional Approach to Technical Harmonisation: Accomplishment and Deficiencies', in Pelkmans and Vanheuklen, eds., *Coming to Grips with the Internal Market*, pp. 9–30. European Institute of Public Administration, Maastricht, 1985.

[17] T. Garvey, 'The New Commission Proposals on Harmonisation of Technical Regulations', ibid, pp. 69–78.

[18] Commission of the EC, *Documents relating to the European Monetary System*, European Economy, no. 12, 1982.

[19] Monetary Committee of the EC, *Compendium of Community Monetary Texts.* Luxemburg, 1986.

[20] Commission of the EC, *The European Community's Budget.* Brussels, 1986.

[21] D. Strasser, *The Finances of Europe.* European Perspectives, Commission of the EC, 1980.

[22] Commission of the EC, *Making a Success of the Single Act: A New Frontier for Europe*, COM (87)100. Feb. 1987.

[23] P. Geroski and A. Jacquemin, *Industrial Change, Barriers to Mobility, and European Industrial Policy*. Economic Policy no. 1, 1985.

[24] J. Pelkmans, *Competing the internal market for industrial products*. (shortened version of the Netherlands Scientific Council's report *De Interne EC Markt voor industriële produkten*). Commission of the EC, Luxemburg, 1986.

[25] F. Cooper, *Pre-conditions for the Emergence of a European Common Market in Armaments*. CEPS Papers, no. 18, Centre for European Policy Studies, Brussels, 1985.

[26] M. King, *The Cash Flow Corporate Income Tax*. Taxation Incentives and the Distribution of Income, Discussion Paper no. 95, London School of Economics, 1986.

[27] S. Krislov, C. D. Ehlermann, and J. Weiler, *The Political Organs and the Decision-making Process in the United States and the European Community*. Vol. 1, 2 of *Integration through Law*, ed. Coppelletti, Seccombe, and Weiler. European University Institute, Florence; Walter de Greuyter, Berlin, 1986.

[28] R. Dornbusch, *Open Economy Macroeconomics*. New York, 1980.

[29] F. Giavazzi and M. Pagano, *The Advantage of Tying One's Hands: EMS Discipline and Central Bank Credibility*. Centre for Economic Policy Research, London, 1986.

[30] M. Albert, *Un pari pour l'Europe*. Paris, 1983.

[31] D. MacDougall, *The Role of Public Finance in European Economic Integration*, Vols. 1 and 2. Commission of the EC, 1977.

[32] J. Paelinck *et al.*, *Formal Spatial Economic Analysis*. Aldershot, 1982.

[33] Commission of the EC, *Perspectives for the Common Agricultural Policy [Green Paper]*. Brussels, 1985.

[34] L. Spaventa *et al.*, *The Future of Community Finance*. Centre for European Policy Studies, Brussels, 1986.

[35] Commission of the EC, *Report by the Commission to the Council and Parliament on the Financing of the Community Budget*, COM (87)101. Brussels, 1987.

[36] Commission of the EC, *Annual Economic Report 1985–86*. European Economy no. 26, Nov. 1985.

[37] Commission of the EC, *Annual Economic Report 1986–87*. European Economy no. 30, Nov. 1986.

[38] H. Reichenbach, 'Les Déséquilibres des flux budgétaires', *Revue francaise des finances publiques*, 4 (1983).

[39] H. Reichenbach, 'EC Budgetary Imbalances: A Conceptual Framework'. *Finanzarchiv*, 41/3 (1983).

[40] Commission of the EC, *Study Group on the Economic Integration Strategy of the Community*, Press Release IP (86) 533.

Annexes

A
Economic Integration in Europe: Some Conceptual Issues
by Paul Krugman

This paper presents a brief, non-technical survey of current thinking about the economics of international economic integration, with an emphasis on concepts relevant to European problems. The paper is intended to be useful in thinking both about those moves toward closer integration of the long-standing members of the EC envisaged under the heading of 'completion of the internal market' and to the issues presented by EC enlargement. Thus, the paper reviews not only the implications of international trade but the effect of integration of capital and labour markets as well.

Some of the effects of international economic integration are familiar, part of the common currency of economic discussion. International trade increases world efficiency by allowing countries to specialize in activities in which they are relatively productive, or that use intensively their relatively abundant resources. International factor mobility, whether of capital or labour, similarly raises world efficiency by transferring resources to countries where their marginal product is higher. On the other hand, both trade and factor mobility may have strong effects on income distribution, so that the owners of initially scarce factors—which become less scarce as a result of increased integration—may be left worse off despite gains for the nation as a whole. And the process of adjustment to increased integration may be difficult, involving temporary unemployment of labour or capital.

These effects of integration are well known. The need for a new survey of the economics of integration arises from the growing recognition that there are other effects as well. Much recent work in international economics has been driven by the perception of more complex consequences of economic integration than conventional accounts describe. These additional consequences arise from two sources. First, the *microeconomics* of international markets are now seen as more complex than the conventional view had recognized. Second, international integration has *macroeconomic* consequences that have only recently been fully appreciated.

This paper is in three parts. The first part reviews the microeconomics of international economic integration, with emphasis on the relatively new issues that arise from the interaction between integration and industrial organization. The second part reviews the macroeconomic consequences of integration, with special emphasis on the co-ordination issues that have been the focus of recent work. Finally, the third part of the paper briefly discusses the policy implications: how might the prospects for successful integration be improved using instruments available to the European Community?

1. Microeconomics of integration

There are some common themes in the microeconomics of international integration, whether this integration takes place through trade in goods, capital movement, or labour mobility. First, integration offers countries an opportunity to benefit from their differences, reallocating resources both domestically and internationally to more productive uses. Second, integration offers further opportunities for gains from increased competition and rationalization to realize economies of scale and scope. Third, integration also poses problems of adjustment and income distribution.

Although these themes are common to all forms of integration, however, the institutional and regulatory framework differs considerably among trade in goods, capital, and labour. Thus we consider each form of integration separately.

1.1 Integration of goods markets

1.1.1 Comparative advantage and the conventional analysis

The most basic analysis of the effects of international trade in goods and services has not changed in its essentials since Ricardo expressed the principle of comparative advantage in the early nineteenth century. Countries trade because they are different; each country specializes in activities in which it is relatively efficient, or which use intensively its relatively abundant resources. This specialization raises the efficiency of the world economy as a whole and produces mutual benefits to the trading nations.

Although new developments in the analysis of international trade, described below, have modified this view, the insights from conventional trade theory remain important. In particular, the basic comparative advantage approach to trade is useful to keep in check two fallacies that remain common in popular discussion, and that could easily cloud understanding of the implications of EC enlargement.

The first misconception is that integration is only beneficial to a country if that country is able to achieve productivity comparable to that of its trading partners. That is, the popular concern is that a country will be hurt by enlarged trade if it is too inefficient to be 'competitive'. What the concept of comparative advantage makes clear is that absolute productivity advantage in some areas is not necessary for a country to gain from integration. Even a country that is less productive than its trading partners across the board can gain by specializing in those sectors in which its productivity disadvantage is smallest. 'Competitiveness' is not a long run, microeconomic issue. To the extent that international competitiveness is a legitimate concern, it is a short-run macroeconomic issue of the kind addressed in the second part of this paper.

The second misconception that conventional analysis helps to dispel is the other side of the same coin. This is the fear that international competition will be harmful if it is based on lower wages rather than higher productivity. Again, the concept of comparative advantage makes it clear that gains from integration do not depend on parity in wage rates. A highly productive country may be more efficient than its trading partners in almost everything, yet it can still gain by specializing in its areas of greatest relative productivity while importing goods in which its productivity advantage is smaller from less productive, and hence lower-wage, nations.

The basic comparative advantage analysis, then, remains important and useful. It has become increasingly clear from recent research, however, that comparative advantage by itself is not an adequate explanation of international trade. This is perhaps especially true of trade within Europe. Thus it is necessary to turn to more recent and less familiar concepts.

1.1.2 Increasing returns and imperfect competition[1]

The need to extend the comparative advantage approach to international trade arises from two related observations:

1. *Much trade occurs because of economies of scale rather than comparative advantage.* When there are advantages to large-scale production, costs will be reduced by concentrating production of each good in a single location. Concentration of production would, however, require international specialization and trade even if countries were identical in productivity and resources. In practice, it seems likely that much of the trade in manufactured goods between the advanced nations of Europe (like much of the inter-regional trade within North America) represents specialization to realize economies of scale rather than a response to national differences in technology or resources. This conclusion is based on two observations. First, there is the evident similarity in the countries' economic bases (is Germany or France more capital-abundant?). Second, there is the high incidence of 'intra-industry' trade, i.e. two-way trade in goods produced using similar technologies and similar mixes of factor inputs.

The importance of increasing returns in international markets has an important implication for the structure of these markets, which leads to the second key departure from the conventional comparative advantage approach:

2. *Many international markets are oligopolistic rather than perfectly competitive.* An inevitable consequence of economies of scale is that markets for manufactured goods are rarely composed of a large number of firms. Each of these firms is aware that its actions have an effect on world prices; in many markets, each

---

[1] The theory of international trade in the presence of increasing returns and imperfect competition has experienced explosive growth since the late 1970s. Much of this work is surveyed and synthesized in E. Helpman and P. Krugman, *Market Structure and Foreign Trade: Increasing Returns, Imperfect Competition, and the International Economy*, MIT Press, 1985.

firm produces goods that are sufficiently differentiated from those of its rivals that it is in fact able to set its own prices. The price-setting ability of firms is, however, constrained by competition; the intensity of this competition depends, among other things, on the extent to which national markets are integrated.

The recognition of the related importance of increasing returns and imperfect competition in international markets requires some modification of the analysis of the effects of increased economic integration. Probably the most important consequence for our thinking is that additional gains from integration become apparent. Against these newly appreciated sources of gains, however, must be set the perception of some risks of adverse consequences of trade liberalization.

The direct source of gains from integration that becomes apparent in the light of new models of international trade is that of increased efficiency when trade allows 'rationalization' to realize economies of scale. The point is perhaps best made by example. When the US and Canada liberalized trade in automotive goods in the mid-1960s, the Canadian industry was able to specialize in producing a narrower range of products while maintaining employment through exports. This allowed Canadian auto production to take place for the first time at a scale and efficiency comparable to that of the US. At least at first, the trade in automotive products was roughly balanced; that is, there was little of the inter-industry reallocation of resources associated with conventional gains from trade. Thus the gains from the auto pact represented extra benefits over and above those captured by conventional analyses.

In addition to the direct gains in efficiency associated with rationalization of production, integration can also have a benign effect on oligopolistic markets by increasing competition. Economies of scale that bulk large relative to any national market, and would therefore lead inevitably to highly concentrated industries at the national level, may be much smaller relative to the EC market as a whole. Thus economic integration may in effect serve as an anti-trust policy, curbing what would otherwise be problematic levels of monopoly power.

A recognition of the role of increasing returns and imperfect competition, then, offers extra reasons to expect benefits from moves toward greater integration of goods markets. Indeed, an emphasis on these additional gains is an important feature of current policy discussion in North America. Canadian economists have stressed scale economies and imperfect competition as reasons to move to free trade with the United States. An influential effort to quantify the benefits of North American free trade, by Richard Harris of Queen's University, suggests that the competition/scale gains for Canada would be more than twice as large as the gains from conventional comparative advantage.[2]

[2] R. Harris and D. Cox, *Trade, Industrial Policy, and Canadian Manufacturing*, University of Toronto Press, 1984.

Unfortunately, while scale economies and oligopoly increase the *potential* gains from trade, they also open up some possible ways in which trade can have adverse effects. The negative aspects have received considerable attention recently, and thus require discussion.

1.1.3 Potential adverse effects of trade[3]

With growing discussion of the role of imperfect competition in trade, certain possibilities of adverse results have been noted. Most of the concern focuses on the possibility that the benefits of international integration will be divided unevenly, with some countries possibly emerging as net losers. This concern is sharpened by the possibility that nationalistic policies could be used to secure benefits for one country at the expense of others. Finally, there are at least in theory ways in which all parties could end up worse off as a result of trade liberalization.

The possibility of uneven distribution of benefits is associated with the existence of excess returns in imperfectly competitive industries. In industries where economies of scale limit the extent of competition, capital can earn a return higher than it does in alternative uses. (If labour is organized, some of this return may be captured in wages instead). A country that succeeds in getting a disproportionate share of high-return industries as a result of trade can gain at other countries' expense, while a country that ends up with small high-return sectors can conceivably be worse off with trade than without.

While the possibility of actual losses from trade is probably purely academic, there is a real issue of conflict over the division of the gains. Because some industries yield higher returns than others, countries have an incentive to take unilateral measures to secure a larger share of these sectors. Policies aimed at securing national advantage in oligopolistic industries have come to be known as *strategic* trade policies. Recent efforts to quantify the possible scope for such policies suggests that it may be in the national interest to impose tariffs or provide export subsidies at rates as high as 20–30 per cent in selected sectors.[4]

The problem is that while strategic trade policies may be in any one country's interest, if all countries pursue them the result may be to block mutually beneficial integration. Suppose that semiconductors are viewed as a

---

[3] The possibility that countries can use subsidies and other policies to secure a higher share of excess-return industries was pointed out by James Brander and Barbara Spencer in 'International R&D Rivalry and Industrial Strategy', *Review of Economic Studies*, 50 (1983), 707–22, and in their 'Export Subsidies and International Market Share Rivalry', *Journal of International Economics*, 18 (1985), 83–100. The implications of the Brander–Spencer analysis and critiques of its relevance as a guide to policy are covered in many of the papers in P. Krugman, ed., *Strategic Trade Policy and the New International Economics*, MIT Press, 1986.

[4] See in particular A. Dixit, 'Optimal Trade and Industrial Policy for the US Automobile Industry', forthcoming in R. Feenstra, ed., *Empirical Research in International Trade*, MIT Press; R. Baldwin and P. Krugman, 'Market Access and Competition: A Simulation Study of 16K random access memories', forthcoming in the same volume; and A. Venables and M. A. M. Smith, 'Trade and Industrial Policy Under Imperfect Competition', *Economic Policy*, 3, 1986.

strategic sector suitable for special government attention. A single country could then gain by promoting this industry. If every major nation attempts to ensure a strong position in semiconductors through protection and subsidies, however, the outcome will be a fragmented high-cost industry, which benefits no country.

Under the rules of the EC, of course, direct use of protectionist measures with regard to intra-EC trade is ruled out. Indirect measures such as nationalistic procurement and government support of industry, subsidized R&D, and so on can still, however, have similar, although more muted effects. Thus the problem of an industrial policy war that blocks beneficial integration remains a serious concern.

We should also note that since Europe does not trade only with itself, but is also engaged in trade and competition with other regions, European integration itself is a kind of strategic trade policy. Theoretical models of strategic trade policy show that in industries subject to increasing returns, the size of the domestic market can be an important determinant of export performance. Again, recent efforts at quantification provide some support for this view, especially for high technology sectors. Thus, increasing the degree of integration of the European market may produce 'strategic' gains over and above the usual benefits by giving European firms a better base for oligopolistic competition against US and Japanese rivals.

Finally, we should note that in imperfectly competitive markets it is possible in principle that increased integration could leave everyone worse off. The simplest example is the case known as 'reciprocal dumping': oligopolistic firms may restrict sales in their local markets in an effort to keep prices high, while selling at much lower margins in their rivals' markets in pursuit of additional profits. This practice can lead to shipments of the same good in opposite directions, with a consequent waste of resources in transportation costs. If this waste is not outweighed by the gains from increased competition, everyone will be made worse off when markets are integrated.

It remains true, however, that the most likely effect of economies of scale and imperfect competition is to *raise* the gains from integration, and that the major concern is the problem of policy conflict, not direct losses from the integration itself.

1.1.4 Adjustment costs and income distribution

A major obstacle to increased economic integration is the fact that the gains from integration are not shared equally within countries, at least in the short run. The owners of scarce factors of production may command a higher return before trade liberalization than after—one need only mention farmers threatened by low-cost agricultural imports or low-skill workers. Furthermore, it takes time for resources to shift from one sector to another, so that even some of those who stand to gain from integration in the long run may lose at first.

There are three main issues that need to be addressed when we consider the role of adjustment costs and uneven distribution of gains in economic integration. First is the question of whether the costs are purely distributional or represent a net cost to the economy as a whole; if they are purely distributional they do not provide an argument for limiting integration or slowing its pace. Second is the question whether future trade liberalization is likely to present more or less of an adjustment problem than past. Finally, there is the policy question of how to manage adjustment—but this question we reserve for the last part of the paper.

Economic work of the past decade has made it clear that costly adjustment *by itself* does not mean that increased economic integration is of doubtful benefit. It is of course costly for labour and capital to shift from old into new industries. Since these factors have the choice of remaining put, however, their decision to incur the costs of moving can be viewed as a kind of investment project, one in which there need be no divergence between private and and social returns. The costs incurred by factors of production in shifting out of import-competing industries and into new export sectors following a liberalization of trade may therefore be viewed as productive, similar in ultimate effects to the investment needed to take advantage of a new technology. On this view, the costs suffered by workers and firms in industries hurt by trade liberalization are comparable in significance to the losses suffered by buggy manufacturers with the coming of the automobile: distributional effects deserving of compensation, but not a reason to prevent or delay change.

Adjustment costs provide an argument against trade liberalization only if they involve some social cost beyond changes in income distribution. The most important of these would be unemployment. If increased integration leads to a net increase in involuntary unemployment, this may provide a case against moving too fast.

It is not hard to devise stories in which liberalized trade may create unemployment. Suppose, for example, that labour is immobile between sectors and that real wages are rigid downward but not upward. Suppose also that trade liberalization increases the demand for labour in sectors that were already prosperous, while reducing it in sectors that were already suffering high unemployment. (For example, trade liberalization might benefit Southern England while hurting the North.) Then in the prosperous sectors the effect will be mostly a rise in real wages rather than in employment, while in the declining sectors real wages will fail to fall and unemployment will rise. The net effects will therefore be a fall in employment, possibly negating the benefits of integration.

This story need not be right, of course. If even relatively well off sectors have substantial unemployment, they can experience large job gains. For that matter, trade liberalization could benefit high-unemployment sectors at the expense of low-unemployment ones. None the less, the possibility that adjustment costs can turn into real social costs should not be lightly dismissed.

Given that adjustment represents a definite political problem and at least potentially a real cost to the economy, how much adjustment will increased integration require? Here the important point is that the EEC's past experience has been one of increased integration with remarkably easy adjustment. This will unfortunately not necessarily be true in the future.

In its original formation, the Common Market was virtually tailor-made to foster *intra*-industry trade based on economies of scale rather than *inter*-industry specialization that might have posed large adjustment issues. The original Six were all more or less advanced industrial countries (if we exclude the south of Italy), with similar levels of productivity, wages, and capital–labour ratios. Thus the specialization that took place as trade in manufactured goods grew tended to involve concentration on different niches within sectors rather than wholesale concentration of different countries on different industries. Essentially, all of the growth in intra-EC manufactures trade from 1958 to the mid-1960s took the form of intra- rather than inter-industry exchanges.

The one sector where large inter-sectoral specialization might have been expected to occur was agriculture. Here, however, the Common Agricultural Policy, by ensuring prices above world levels, protected the agricultural sectors of countries that in fact were at a comparative disadvantage.

In part due to the relatively benign character of the trade expansion it produced, the EEC in its years of rapid trade growth aroused fewer complaints about problems of adjustment than many had expected. The question now is whether the further extension of trade in progress will be equally easy to cope with.

The unfortunate answer is, probably not. To the extent that unification of standards and a reduction in nationalistic purchasing practices can increase trade among the wealthier nations of the enlarged EEC, this may produce a further round of intra-industry specialization with few adjustment costs. The addition of Southern Europe to the scene, however, means that now trade within the EEC will involve partners with major differences in productivity, wages, and resources. Trade between Portugal and Belgium will surely be more conventional in its character than trade between Belgium and Germany; it will involve specialization in labour-intensive, low-technology products by the one and exports of higher-technology, capital- or skill-intensive products by the other. This will pose adjustment problems for both the heretofore protected Portuguese heavy industries and some traditional industries in Northern Europe.

The point is that the trade expansion produced by EC enlargement is simply not likely to be as painless as the trade expansion produced by the formation of the Community and earlier enlargement. There will certainly be income distribution problems created by the changes, and also quite possibly some real costs in terms of unemployment.

1.2 Integration of capital markets

In a deep, underlying sense, integration of national economies through capital movements is not very different in its causes and effects from trade in goods and services. As in the case of trade, capital movements serve to allow countries to benefit from their differences through long-run transfer of resources to countries where they are more productive. Also like trade, capital mobility can be beneficial through its effects on financial market efficiency even where little net transfer of resources takes place. On the other hand, differences in regulation and the institutional framework make the issue of capital controls quite different in practice from the issue of protectionism.

1.2.1 Long-run resource transfer

The use of capital movement to transfer resources is both the most obvious reason for such movements and the most obvious source of gain. By investing abroad, individuals can shift resources to where they are most productive, in principle benefiting both the recipient of the capital inflow (via increased production that exceeds the repayment) and the donor (via higher foreign investment income).

As Robert Mundell pointed out nearly thirty years ago, long-run resource transfer via capital movement may serve as a substitute for international trade, and vice versa. Capital-abundant countries may either trade capital-intensive for labour-intensive goods, or directly trade the services of their capital for a stream of future goods. Either way, the trade allows countries to gain from their differences.

In the era before World War I, long-run resource transfer was the prime reason for capital movement, and took place on a massive scale. The UK invested 5–10 per cent of GNP abroad for decades, and on the eve of the war its foreign investment income paid for a third of its imports. In the 1980s, however, net resource transfer has been much smaller relative to national incomes. In any case, it is doubtful whether moves currently under consideration will do much to increase long-run resource transfer through capital flows. First, most of the regulations restricting capital mobility that are likely to be liberalized bite most strongly on short-run movements rather than long-term capital. Second, the main likely recipients of net foreign investment within the Community (Greece, Ireland) are already sufficiently heavily indebted that further large inflow seems unlikely.

Thus, the main gains from liberalized capital in the European case seem likely to come not from net resource transfer but from the efficiency advantages of a more integrated European capital market. These benefits are harder to define, but they can be described in rough terms.

1.2.2 Integration and efficiency of financial markets

It is useful, in thinking about integration of capital markets, to draw an analogy with trade in goods and services. Long-run resource transfer corresponds to inter-industry trade: it represents trade of one kind of useful object (purchasing power now) for another (purchasing power in the future), and arises because the relative prices of these two objects (the rate of return) would differ between countries in the absence of trade. Thus it allows countries to benefit from their differences, while at the same time generating income distribution and adjustment problems that may be problematic politically.

On the other side, corresponding to the 'intra-industry' trade that we observe in goods markets, is two-way trade in financial assets and the effect of potential financial flows on competition. Two-way international investment is more subtle in its origins than two-way trade in similar goods, but we can at least enumerate a few main causes.

1. *Diversification*. Since risks are not perfectly correlated across countries, investors in an integrated market will have some incentive to diversify across countries. As each country's investors do this, the result will be financial flows in two directions at once.

2. *Intermediation*. International financial centres provide investors with short-term, safe, liquid assets while acquiring long-term, risky, illiquid claims. As other countries trade assets with financial centres, the result is simultaneous flow of capital in both directions. The role of some cities as centres of international intermediation, in turn, may represent a combination of comparative advantage and economies of scale. Most notably, London acts as a world financial centre partly because of the external economies associated with its already established position (which in turn rests on historical accident).

3. *Information*. When financial resources are traded, since nothing material is being shipped, the cost of information rather than physical costs represents the main natural barrier to trade. Often, however, information will flow more easily between geographically separate but economically linked parties than between physical neighbours. A firm in Italy that seeks additional funds may find that its parent company in the Netherlands or a bank familiar with its industry in London is more able to evaluate its needs than potential sources of capital in Italy itself. Yet at the same time, firms in the Netherlands or England may find that the potential sources of funds that are well-enough informed to provide what is necessary are in Italy. Thus the vagaries of information flow may create a 'geography' of capital markets that differs from actual geography enough to generate capital flows in all directions.

4. *Competition*. Even if there is no reason for net trade in capital, integration of capital markets will create the potential for increased competition. If, say, cartelized banks in one country were to attempt to use their market power to drive a wedge between the rates paid to depositors and the rate charged to lenders, foreign competitors could offer more attractive intermediation and hence induce both export and import of capital. The competition between oligopolistic financial institutions in different countries need not involve much actual capital movement, but it might involve some two-way raiding of each

others' territory, along the lines of the 'reciprocal dumping' mentioned earlier as a possible behaviour in goods markets.

The important point is that these effects on financial market efficiency do not depend on the achievement of large net resource flows. Suppose that Italy and France were to remove all of their restrictions on capital movement. They might not end up exporting or importing large amounts of capital on net (indeed we would hope not). None the less, their integration with the open capital markets of Germany and the United Kingdom could produce significant gains from improved prospects for diversification, economies of scale in intermediation, improved ability of firms to pair up with well-informed investors, and increased financial market competition.

Sceptics would argue, however, that financial markets are so distorted by other government policies that the gains from removal of capital controls are in fact highly uncertain. This is an important caveat, which needs some discussion.

1.2.3 Distortions and questions about the benefits of capital mobility

There is no question that financial markets in all countries suffer from significant distortions. These distortions raise the possibility that increased international trade in financial assets could hurt the economy instead of help it, and correspondingly that restrictions on international capital movements may be desirable as a second-best way of mitigating the effects of distortions.

One main set of distortions comes from the moral hazard problems created by bank regulation. The desire to prevent 1930s-style banking collapses has led nearly all nations to provide a safety net of deposit insurance, together with implicit guarantees that the government will bail out the banking system if necessary. These measures are surely desirable: few would advocate a return to complete *laissez-faire*. None the less, they present moral hazard problems. Banks are offered an incentive to take excessive risks, especially risks that offer a low probability of large losses. If the low-probability disasters do not happen, the bank has earned a high return; if they do happen, depositors are protected, while stockholders can at most lose their equity—and may not even lose that, if the government bails them out. An unconditional provision of deposit insurance is in its effect essentially like a government subsidy to risk-taking, and its effect in that direction is reinforced if bank equity is perceived to be subject to implicit guarantees.

Now in fact the explicit and implicit guarantees of governments to the financial system are not unconditional. They are backed by regulations designed to discourage excessive risk-taking, both prudential regulations on exposure and capitalization requirements that insure that bank equity is large enough to bear much of the responsibility of adverse outcomes. The problem is that internationalization of capital markets can weaken the effectiveness of the regulatory framework. For example, some economists have argued that creation of Eurosubsidiaries by US banks during the 1970s reduced the effectiveness of capital requirements, leading banks into a surge of risky lending that produced, among other things, the explosion in LDC debt during 1978–81. Whether or not this was in fact a major factor, it is clear that integration on financial markets requires revision of the regulatory framework. Without such revision, capital flows will be motivated more by a search for loopholes than a search for real economic opportunities, and reduce welfare instead of increasing it.

A second kind of distortion involves taxation. A recurrent theme in practical discussion of international capital movements is that they may take place as a way to avoid taxation. First, the effectiveness of taxation on foreign capital is uncertain; residents of countries with weak fiscal systems may be able to avoid reporting their income on investments outside the country. If it is easier to avoid payment of taxes on foreign income than domestic, which is likely, capital flight will take place without any gain in economic efficiency. Notably, those European countries with capital controls are also those noted for problems with tax collection.

If fiscal problems make seignorage an important source of revenue, the problem is compounded. A country that relies to a significant extent on inflation for revenue will offer a strongly negative real return on its currency, and a low real return on bank deposits (because banks must in effect pay the inflation tax on their required reserves). Suppose that such a country liberalizes capital mobility. Then there will be some decline in the demand for currency, as new substitutes become available; and also a decline in demand for deposits. This will either reduce inflation revenue or force a higher inflation rate on the government. Since the capital flight would have responded to an inflation tax rather than underlying differences in productivity, it may be regarded as capital movement motivated by tax evasion—and it will lower national income, not raise it.

It is hard to deny that in practice problems of taxation and regulation do bulk large in capital markets, making the gains from liberalization problematic. One counter-argument to this counter-argument would be to argue for a capital market integration accompanied by institutional reform that corrects these problems; some ideas along these lines are discussed below. Another argument would be that capital controls themselves create serious distortions of incentives. Capital controls create incentives to engage in activities that are not socially productive, but that serve as ways to evade the controls. For example, if devaluation is anticipated but capital flight is prohibited, consumers may respond by hoarding consumer durables, a costly activity from the point of view of the nation but one that absence of financial alternatives makes profitable.

Also, like any government regulation, capital controls pose problems of enforcement. On one side, illegal activities such as falsified invoicing are difficult to police. On the other side, the regulations that make controls effective may also throw sand in the wheels of valuable economic activities.

When it is necessary to apply for permission to acquire foreign exchange, the ease that facilitates transactions, especially small ones, will be lost.

1.3 Integration of labour markets

Labour mobility, like capital mobility, is similar in its ultimate causes to trade in goods. On one side we have net migration of labour from one country to another, corresponding to inter-industry trade in goods. On the other we have at least the possibility of exchange of labour in a more balanced way, corresponding to intra-industry trade.

1.3.1 Migration as resource transfer

The role of international migration as a means of transferring resources needs little discussion. When workers move from low-wage nations to higher-wage countries their income rises, and so does the income of the recipient nation. World income is increased because labour is being transferred to places where it has a higher marginal product.

The movement of labour from South to North in Europe during the 1960s and 1970s is, of course, one of the great migrations in history. This migration had social and economic consequences that are beyond the scope of this paper. The important point for the current situation is that the EC enlargement has brought some of the major reservoirs of labour inside the EC, and thus will presumably encourage an increase in the future extent of migration.

1.3.2 'Intra-industry' migration

In the United States, which is comparable in population to and much larger in area than the EC, net inter-regional migration flows are accompanied by large two-way flows of people. It is not uncommon for a house in New York to be vacated by a family moving to California, and for the house to be occupied by a family just moving in from California. This two-way migration is not fully understood, but it may be explained by several causes:

1. *Differentiation in skills.* If one region is abundant in skilled labour, while another is abundant in unskilled, two-way migration is not unreasonable. Something of this kind went on during the 1940s and 1950s, when a large net migration of unskilled labour from the Southern US to the North was countered by a smaller migration of skilled workers in the other direction.

2. *Information networks.* This is an explanation similar to our discussion of information as a cause of capital movement. Suppose that a software firm in California needs more programmers with a specific kind of background. There may be programmers with that background in California, but the firm might well find it easier to hire people it knows through personal ties or past business dealings who happen to live in Texas or Massachusetts. The point is again that the 'geography' of information networks may not bear much resemblance to the geography of a map, so that resources several thousand miles away may in effect be more accessible than those in the same city.

3. *Internal labour markets and the operations of large firms*. Suppose that a firm that operates plants and offices in a number of states decides to relocate some of its operations. Often in such a case the firm will try to provide its employees with job security by offering them the opportunity to take jobs in the new location. Thus the firm creates an internal labour market from which it hires in preference to hiring from geographically localized external markets. The reasons for this preference for internal hiring—like the preference for internal financing—presumably at root come down to issues of information and insurance. The point is, however, that it can lead to substantial movement of people in all directions.

The notable feature of European labour markets as compared with those of the US is that so far this kind of two-way migration flow is relatively absent. Presumably this is mostly because of language and cultural barriers. It might also be to some extent because of social policies, e.g. claims on subsidized housing that migrants cannot take with them. An interesting question is whether over time the EC will be able to create a labour market that is integrated in this way, and reap the benefits of increased efficiency.

1.4 Conclusions

For all three forms of economic integration—goods and services, capital, and labour market—the effects of reduced barriers can be usefully divided into two kinds. On one side is the conventional or comparative advantage motive for trade driven by differences in countries' resources or productivity. Trade resulting from this conventional motive produces mutual gains in efficiency, but also produces problems of income distribution and adjustment. On the other side is trade motivated by unconventional factors: economies of scale, oligopolistic rivalry, informational asymmetries, and so on. The trade that these unconventional motives produce is similarly (usually) beneficial; however, it probably involves less conflict of interest *within* countries and more conflict of interest *between* countries than conventional trade.

The problem facing Europe is twofold. First, the expansion of trade that will be generated by the enlargement of the Community will probably involve an expansion of conventional, comparative-advantage specialization. This represents a break with the past history of the EEC, which was so successful in the 1960s at least partly because of the predominance of 'intra-industry' over 'inter-industry' trade. The new trade expansion will thus present problems of internal adjustment that will be of greater difficulty than before.

Second, and working in the other direction, completion of the internal market will sharpen the potential for national conflict over the distribution of the unconventional gains from trade. There are bound to be sectors that are regarded as strategic by several European countries, but which tend to concentrate in only one or two. The danger is then of an industrial policy war as each country attempts to secure the desired sectors for itself.

2. Macroeconomics of integration[5]

The objective of international economic integration is to reap the microeconomic benefits of specialization, rationalization, and increased competition. Unfortunately, microeconomic objectives can never be fully separated from macroeconomic issues. Recent research has suggested that under certain circumstances increased integration can worsen macroeconomic performance (though under other circumstances it might be an advantage).

The reason why macroeconomic problems from integration are possible is that increased integration means increased macroeconomic interdependence. In and of itself this is not a bad thing; the fact that Ohio's economy depends on the performance of New York's does not pose special problems for US monetary and fiscal policy. The difference is that Europe's nations do not have fully co-ordinated policies. What recent research has shown is that increased interdependence without a corresponding increase in co-ordination can lead to inappropriate policies. At worst, the problems of co-ordination could negate the microeconomic benefits of expanded integration. Even if this is not the case, increased integration makes policy co-ordination more urgent.

2.1 Channels of interdependence

As a first step toward thinking about the macroeconomics of integration, it is helpful to review the main channels of interdependence between nations. These are of course interdependence through goods and service markets; linkage of capital markets, which have a particularly strong role in determining exchange rates; and, in Europe, the direct linkage of employment through policy effects on migration.

2.1.1 Trade and its multiplier effects

The simplest form of macroeconomic linkage between countries is the spillover of demand from one country to another via imports. While much of the attention of economists has focused on the more indirect linkages via financial and exchange markets, this direct and straightforward linkage should not be neglected. In Europe more than anywhere else in the world the spill-over of demand between countries is of vital importance. The average Community nation (which turns out to be France, more or less) imports and exports about a quarter of its GDP and has a marginal propensity to import of more than one-third; but about 60 per cent of these imports come from other European countries, so that Europe as a whole is as closed an economy as the United States.

Until recently most of the analytical attention of economists studying trade linkages was focused on the question of foreign trade multipliers: how much

---

[5] Much of the analysis in this section is simply conventional open-economy macroeconomics, as exposited, for example, in R. Dornbusch, *Open-economy Macroeconomics*, Basic Books, 1980.

does a percentage point of growth in Germany affect GDP in France? These numbers are much larger within Europe than, say, between Europe and the US. None the less, emphasis on trade multipliers is now seen to miss the most important point. What matters is not so much how much a given German policy affects France as the way that interdependence affects the policies pursued by both Germany and France. We shall examine this issue soon, but first we continue by discussing the roles of linkage through capital markets and labour markets.

2.1.2 Capital markets, monetary policy, and exchange rates

Integration of capital markets introduces a more complex and less well understood policy linkage than trade in goods and services. The picture is complicated by the question of exchange rate regime. If exchange rates are flexible, capital market linkages operate in the first instance through exchange rate changes. If on the other hand exchange rates are more or less fixed, the integration of capital markets introduces a direct linkage between monetary policy in one country and the money supplies in others.

In the case of flexible rates, anything that raises the rate of return in one country tends to appreciate its currency against its trading partners, while anything that lowers the rate of return in a country tends to depreciate its currency. The more integrated are capital markets, the more pronounced these effects. It is a familiar proposition from international macroeconomics that in a world of high capital mobility, some effects of fiscal and monetary policy may go in unexpected directions. The two main examples are a reversed effect of fiscal expansion on the exchange rate, and a reversed effect of monetary policy on the current account.

If capital markets are not highly integrated, we should expect a fiscal expansion to raise the demand for imports and thus lead to currency depreciation. When capital markets are closely integrated, however, fiscal expansion that drives up interest rates may induce capital inflow that actually produces a currency appreciation. (This effect of course becomes much more likely when the fiscal expansion is accompanied by tightened monetary policy).

On the other side, we might expect that monetary expansion, which raises demand for imports as well as domestic goods, will lead to a current account deficit. With capital mobility and flexible exchange rates, however, monetary expansion may depress the currency so much that a current account surplus emerges instead. (For what it is worth, most econometric models suggest that things are not quite this perverse. Regressive expectations seem to limit the decline in the currency following monetary expansion enough so that the current account worsens after all).

The combination of flexible rates and high capital mobility creates a direct channel whereby each country's monetary policy has a direct—and perverse—effect on its trading partners' inflation. Tight money in one country appreciates its currency, reducing import prices at home but raising them abroad.

When rates are fixed, the effect of increased capital market integration is to remove the possibility of independent national monetary policies. An attempt to pursue seriously divergent policies will lead to capital flows that cannot for long be offset by sterilized intervention, and eventually one country or the other will have to allow its money supply to be dictated by the other country's.

2.1.3 Labour market linkage

There is not much deep to say about the direct role of labour market integration in creating economic linkages. Clearly, reduced employment in Northern Europe swells unemployment in Southern Europe, as migrants return home and potential migrants choose not to go. In general we might expect migrant employment to be more sensitive to economic fluctuations than overall employment; even with the protection of common EEC labour law, migrants will tend to find themselves in the position of 'last hired, first fired'. The significance of this is that looking at absolute numbers employed may understate the true importance of the linkage. Suppose that one worker in ten in Northern Europe were from Southern Europe, and the one Southerner in ten worked in the North. Then the extent of labour market integration might not seem very large. But if Southerners are in effect the reserve army that fills fluctuations in Northern demand, the marginal propensity to hire Southerners will be much higher than the average. An extra ten Northern jobs might translate into several jobs for Southerners, not just one.

2.2 Policy problems posed by interdependence

The essential policy problem posed by interdependence is that policies that affect residents of each nation are made at least in part by governments of other nations. This can lead to two sorts of bad result. First, a failure of governments to predict correctly what others' actions will be can lead to increased uncertainty and volatility in economic policy. Second, there may be a problem of collective action, in which rational policies from the point of view of governments acting on their own sum up to inferior policies at the level of Europe as a whole.

2.2.1 Information and uncertainty

Suppose that France and Germany set their macroeconomic policies independently, and that there is enough of a lag in the policy process that each country must base its policy on a guess about the other's future policy rather than responding to the actual policy adopted. Then uncertainty about the other country's policy can clearly be a problem. If France decides to expand when Germany decides to contract, France may end up with a bigger trade deficit than it bargained on. If France decides to contract, not realizing that Germany has made the same decision, both countries will be surprised at the depth of the recession that results.

This is not just an academic concern. Many observers, including the OECD secretariat, have argued that the severity of the 1982 slump in part reflected just such a failure to forecast other countries' actions. As many countries turned toward restrictive demand policies at the same time, each failed to appreciate how much its export demand would fall as a result of the actions taken abroad. The consequence was a deeper slump than anyone intended. We might also argue that some abrupt U-turns in policy—France being the obvious example—were prompted in part by the initial failure to predict correctly other countries' macroeconomic policies.

If information and uncertainty were the only problem posed by increased interdependence, the solution could lie in a more extensive process of mutual notification. It has become clear in recent years, however, that there are deeper issues of co-ordination that cannot be resolved simply by information exchange.

2.2.2 Co-ordination issues[6]

The essential co-ordination problem is that when interdependence is high, policies that appear advantageous to any one country acting alone may yield poor results when everyone follows them.

The classic example that has attracted a great deal of academic attention is that of how quickly to attempt to disinflate. Suppose that a number of countries have 'inherited' inflation, either as the result of adverse supply shocks or misguided past policies. Suppose also that exchange rates are freely floating. Then to any individual country a policy of rapid disinflation through restrictive monetary policy may appear attractive. Where capital mobility is high, tight money will lead to a large currency appreciation, and this appreciation will at least at first produce a rapid fall in inflation in a highly open economy. Thus the trade-off between reducing inflation and increasing unemployment may appear relatively favourable. (The trade-off will be even more attractive if many of those who lose their jobs are migrant workers rather than national citizens.) So where markets for goods, capital, and labour are well integrated, each country may find that rapid disinflation through tight money is an appealing strategy.

The problem is that if every country pursues this strategy, the results will not be nearly as favourable. All countries cannot simultaneously experience

---

[6] The discussion in this area is summarized in R. Cooper, 'Economic Interdependence and Co-ordination of Economic Policies', in R. Jones and P. Kenen, eds., *Handbook of International Economics*, North-Holland, 1985. An attempt to quantify the gains from co-ordination is G. Oudiz and J. Sachs, *Macroeconomic policy co-ordination among the Industrial Countries*, Brookings Papers on Economic Activity, 1 (1984).

currency appreciation; if they all pursue equally tight monetary policies, none of them will experience much appreciation. Thus, the cheap gains against inflation will be lost.

One might expect that given the failure to experience rapid disinflation, countries would then choose not to use such tight monetary policies. Once the rest of the world has tight money, however, looser money in one country will imply currency *depreciation*, and a risk of accelerating inflation. In other words, the world can get caught in a trap in which all countries are pursuing more restrictive policies than are in their collective interest, yet no one country will gain from being more expansionary.

Once one realizes that co-ordination problems of this kind can arise, it becomes clear that increased economic integration can aggravate them. The more integrated goods markets are, the greater the inflation gains from appreciation and the greater the inflationary impact of depreciation. The more integrated are capital markets, the greater the extent to which monetary policy acts through the exchange rate rather than through interest-sensitive domestic spending. The more integrated are labour markets, the less of a reduction in employment will be borne by permanent domestic residents.

Because increased interdependence can worsen the problems of co-ordination, a move toward increased integration *if not accompanied by an improved framework for co-ordination* could backfire. Worse macro policy could outweigh the microeconomic gains.

The problem of excessive disinflation under flexible rates is, as we mentioned, the most analysed example of co-ordination problems in recent economic work. It is of doubtful direct relevance to Europe at the present time, however. Inflation is less of a concern than it was; furthermore, much of Europe is now either part of the European Monetary System or increasingly adopting exchange rate targets that link it more or less closely to the EMS. Nonetheless, the co-ordination problem can easily reappear in other guises.

Suppose, for example, that we stylize the European situation now as follows: monetary policy is committed to defense of the exchange rate, but fiscal policy remains available as a macroeconomic tool. Fiscal expansion is constrained, however, by a number of factors including concern over its effect on the currency account balance and concern over long-run government solvency. In this situation it is possible that uncoordinated policies could lead to fiscal policies that are more conservative than optimal. For any one country acting alone, fiscal expansion will largely spill over into imports, so that the adverse current account consequences will be large. At the same time the multiplier effects on domestic output will be small, so that little new tax revenue will be generated and the budget consequences will also be unfavourable. If all Europe expanded at once, however, the current account consequences would be less than half as large for the typical country, the multiplier effects will be larger, and hence the budget impact less unfavourable. Thus countries acting in an uncoordinated fashion would be trapped in a fiscal stance that is tighter than their own interests warrant.

In this case, as in the case of excessive disinflation, increased integration and the resulting interdependence can worsen uncoordinated policy. As goods markets become more integrated, the fraction of an increase in demand that spills over to imports rises. Increased integration of capital markets reinforces the reliance on fiscal as opposed to monetary policy. Increased labour mobility makes extra employment seem less valuable to any one country, even though it is as important as ever to Europe as a whole.

2.3 Macroeconomic advantages of integration

The preceding discussion stressed the problems of macroeconomic policy that can arise from increased economic interdependence. These problems have attracted the most attention from economists. Recent work, however, especially in Europe, has stressed some advantages that macro policy can derive from closer integration. These fall under two headings: the use of the rest of the world as a buffer, and the use of external constraints as a way to gain policy credibility.

2.3.1 Interdependence as a buffer

An open economy is exposed to shocks originating in the outside world, but it is to some extent protected from its own shocks. An investment slump will not produce as much a recession if it falls partly on imports. Under fixed exchange rates, shocks originating in shifts in the demand for money or other portfolio shifts may emerge as capital movements with little real effect, whereas in a closed economy they could have generated real output disturbances.

Will the gain from using the rest of the world as a buffer outweigh the cost of exposing oneself to the rest of the world's variability? There is a presumption that the net effect will be to reduce volatility. If we think of Europe as a collection of countries experiencing imperfectly correlated disturbances to private demand, bouts of governmental irresponsibility, and so on, we can expect the *average* of Europe to show less instability than any one country. But each country's rest of Europe is simply an average of the other countries. So there probably is some useful buffering effect of increased integration.

2.3.2 External discipline and credibility

The more important potential source of macroeconomic gains from integration is its hoped-for ability to enhance the credibility of economic policies. For some time, economists have emphasized the importance of public expectations in economic behaviour. Often it is very difficult for a government to carry out a desired change in economic policy if the public does not believe that the change will last. Most notably, stopping inflation is much more difficult both in fiscal terms and in terms of its output cost when the government's determination is questionable.

In situations where credibility is important, it is often useful to restrict one's own freedom of action. Italy, with its history of inflation, would like to convince both the purchasers of government debt and price setters that it will be much less inflationary in the future. Simple declarations that things will be different from now on are not likely to achieve this goal. In order to gain credibility, the Italian government may therefore wish to constrain its own actions. The hope is that by adopting an exchange rate target *vis-à-vis* a country with less inflation propensity, the government of a high-inflation country can make further inflation too costly—and thereby make its announced intention to pursue price stability credible.

Clearly, such a policy works only if it works. That is, making exchange rate adjustment costly is only a good thing if it actually changes both government policy and expectations enough so that the need for exchange rate adjustment is in fact substantially reduced. Otherwise the only effect is to make the inevitable exchange rate changes come too infrequently, and to create targets for speculative attack. The experience of the EMS so far, and the revealed preferences of European governments at the present time, suggest that external discipline can indeed enhance credibility in a significant way.

The impact of increased integration of markets on the credibility problem is double-edged. On one side, increased integration increases the discipline associated with the external constraint. On the other side, if credibility is not established, the costs of that failure are larger with more open markets.

The case is clearest for capital mobility. A country with effective capital controls can for at least a while pursue an inflationary monetary policy without being forced into an immediate devaluation. By contrast, with free movement of capital it could not. It is fairly common now to hear from French sources that 'we now allow our monetary policy to be made by the Bundesbank'. This has however not been quite true as long as French capital markets have been isolated by controls. Once the controls are gone, if France remains in the EMS, it will be fully true. If the commitment to the EMS remains ironclad, there will thus be a gain in credibility.

On the other hand, suppose that the commitment is not seen as ironclad. Then the opening of capital markets presents opportunities for speculative attack. An extreme example may make the point. In 1981–2 both Brazil and Mexico were following unsustainable policies. Brazil had effective capital controls in place, Mexico did not. Mexico experienced capital flight in excess of $20 billion, which was financed by additional debt, while Brazil's capital flight problem was negligible. If credibility is not gained, there is a good deal to be said for *not* having integrated markets.

2.4 Conclusions

Increased integration makes countries more interdependent in their macroeconomic policies. European nations are already strongly linked through trade, but their labour and especially capital market linkages can still be extended.

Increased interdependence creates problems for macroeconomic policy. Failure of countries to communicate effectively about their intentions can lead to increased uncertainty and policy volatility. More important, there is usually a divergence between the policies that are best for each country acting individually and the policies that would be best if countries acted in a coordinated way. Increased integration can widen this divergence, possibly leading to macroeconomic problems that outweigh the microeconomic gains.

Against these macroeconomic difficulties we can set two gains. Integration can serve as a buffer against uncertainty; for example, fluctuations in money demand will do less harm if they can be averaged across an integrated European capital market. At a deeper level, integration enhances the ability of countries to appeal to external discipline as a way to enhance the credibility of their policies.

3. Policy implications

It is beyond the scope of this paper (and beyond the author's competence!) to make any kind of detailed recommendations for Europe based upon this very general survey. The most that can be done is to outline a few broad concerns for policy as European integration increases.

3.1 Microeconomic policy

3.1.1 Avoiding conflict over industrial structure

The main danger suggested by the 'new theories' of economic integration discussed in the first part of this paper is that nations will find themselves in an industrial policy war, as each attempts to enlarge its share of high-return sectors. The issue is how to structure rules of the game that prevent procurement, subsidies, and other policies from being turned to this purpose and thus frustrating the goal of increased integration.

Now it is notable that the United States, a highly integrated market with a federal system of government, is relatively free of this kind of conflict. Every state would like to have its own Silicon Valley or Route 128, but the policies they follow towards this end have not noticeably disrupted the free flow of goods and services.

How is conflict avoided? We might note five factors that restrain industrial policy conflict within the US.

1. *Constitutional limitations.* States are forbidden from actions in restraint of inter-state trade, ruling out many barriers that would be legal even in the EEC.

2. *Much procurement is carried out at the federal rather than state level.* While states provide education and other services, a good deal of the procurement in potentially strategic sectors is carried out at a Federal level, most notably defence spending.

3. *Firms have much less of a local identification than in Europe.* Digital Equipment Corporation is a Massachusetts-based company, but the state is aware that the firm is truly inter-state in scope and does not automatically regard it as a state champion that needs to be supported against New York-based IBM.

4. *There is extensive redistribution among states through the federal budget.* States are therefore somewhat cushioned from adverse industrial shifts.

5. *Labour mobility is high.* If a large number of high-wage jobs are created in a state, they are as likely as not to be filled by migrants rather than by local residents.

Europe cannot fully reproduce the US situation. Political union is not on the table; and even if it were, the greater cultural and language diversity would prevent comparable integration. None the less, at least four of these five restraints on industrial policy competition can be institutionalized to some extent. 'Completion of the internal market' is very similar as a slogan to 'no restraints on inter-state commerce', and could be used as a principle to achieve the same end. Rules of the game on procurement, and perhaps some explicit co-operation in the defence area, could reduce the segmenting effect of national bias in this area. Liberalization of capital markets, and in particular of rules regarding direct foreign investment, could help make corporations truly European and thus not the special concern of individual nations. Finally, the EC's own redistributive mechanisms can help reduce concerns about losing out from competition, especially for poorer areas.

3.1.2 Promoting better adjustment

It is obvious but worth saying that all the problems associated with greater economic integration, and all the risks of policy conflict, would be far less if the European unemployment rate were half its current level. There is debate about the relative importance of inadequate demand and structural rigidities in causing the current high rate, a debate that should not be joined here. The point is, however, that integration will be far more successful if other policies are simultaneously doing something about the highly unsatisfactory performance of European labour markets.

3.2 Macroeconomic policies

3.2.1 Monetary policy

As a simple matter of feasibility, Europe cannot have at the same time (a) stable exchange rates, (b) integrated capital markets, and (c) independent monetary policies. The experience of the post-1973 period seems to indicate that (a) is not something that can be dispensed with. Given the already close integration of European markets for goods and services, large exchange rate fluctuations associated with divergent monetary policies seem to be unacceptable. Thus creation of a unified capital market will also require adoption of a common monetary policy.

To an outside observer, it appears that this is in fact happening, but not in the most desirable way. It is not too much of a caricature to say that Europe—including the UK!—is starting to look like a Deutschmark area, in which the Bundesbank sets all of Europe's monetary policy. This makes stable exchange rates feasible. The question is whether the arrangement is durable. As long as the need for external discipline to establish credibility is paramount in the minds of the rest of Europe, German centrality works; if and when other considerations become more urgent, the stage may be set for a Bretton Woods-like collapse.

A more desirable arrangement would involve co-operative setting of monetary targets. The difficulties involved in such a project are of course large, but it seems necessary. Though Germany is the largest economy and has a reputation for sound money, it is hard to believe that it is large or sound enough to be ceded control over Europe's money forever.

3.2.2 Fiscal policy

Finally, we turn to fiscal policy. Given mobile capital, it is technically feasible for European nations to maintain fixed exchange rates via co-ordinated monetary policy while pursuing independent fiscal policies. As already noted, however, independent fiscal actions in such a setting may yield suboptimal results—for example, a bias towards excessive restriction because each country ignores the impact of its actions on the others' exports. Given how large European interdependence is already, the further increase in this interdependence makes co-ordination urgent.

Achieving co-ordination of fiscal policies is probably even harder politically than co-ordination of monetary policies. There is not even temporarily a natural central player whose actions can solve the co-ordination problem. None the less, in surveying the problems of European integration, it is hard to avoid the conclusion that this is the systemic change most needed in the near future.

B

The Cash Flow Corporation Tax
by Mervyn King

The principle underlying the cash flow corporation tax is that the company is taxed on the net cash flow received from its real business activities. No distinction is made between capital and income in the calculation of a company's tax base. By basing the tax on cash flow the measurement of economic income is removed from the concern of the tax authorities. Such a system achieves fiscal neutrality by harmonizing investment incentives on a common basis, namely immediate expensing of all investment expenditure. The motivation for the cash flow tax is to apply the principles of a consumption or expenditure tax to the corporate sector. The idea can be traced back at least as far as 1948[1] and discussion of its practical implementations has been raised several times in the past decade.[2]

The cash flow corporate income tax represents an attempt to design a tax that is neutral with respect to both financial and investment decisions, and at the same time continues to yield the government positive revenue from past investments, from profits in excess of the normal rate of return, and also from activities financed by overseas investors. It is attractive for a further reason—namely, that the base of the tax requires no adjustment for inflation; hence, the complicated indexation provisions for depreciation, for example, required under alternative corporate tax systems, are unnecessary with a cash flow tax. This is because the tax is based on the sources and uses of funds statement and not the profit and loss account. The tax eliminates the necessity of calculating 'economic profit'. Hence there is no need to construct a true measure of depreciation nor to make any adjustment for the effects of inflation.

The basic principle of the tax is to levy a charge on the net cash flow to the company resulting from its real economic activities. The tax base can be measured as the difference between the receipts from sales of goods and services and the purchases of all real goods and services required in the production process, including purchases of capital goods. At the same time the tax base would disallow any deduction for the financing of the investment. Hence there would be no deductibility of either interest payments nor dividends. The major departures from present systems would be the granting

[1] H. J. Aaron and H. Galper, *Assessing Tax Reform*, Brookings Institution, Washington DC, 1985.
[2] E. C. Brown, 'Business-income Taxation and Investment Incentives', in *Income, Employment, and Public Policy: Essays in Honor of Alvin H. Hansen*, W. W. Norton, New York, 1984; J. A. Kay and M. A. King, *The British Tax System*, 4th edn., Oxford University Press, 1986; M. A. King, 'Current Policy Problems in Business Taxation', in *Bedrifts Beskatning*, Norwegian School of Economics, Bergen, 1975; Meade Committee *The Structure and Reform of Direct Taxation*, Allen and Unwin, London, 1978.

of immediate expensing (100 per cent first year depreciation allowances) to all forms of investment (but given this there would be no need for an investment tax credit), and interest payments would no longer qualify as a deduction for the purposes of corporate income tax. Dividends would be treated as under the classical system with no imputation relief. In practice, there would need to be transitional arrangements to prevent both undue hardship and also tax avoidance during the transition from the current system to a new cash flow tax base. These are discussed below.

The nature of a double-entry book-keeping means that the total sources of funds to a company are identical to its total uses of funds. An important implication of this identity is that the base of the cash flow tax can be described in either of two ways. The first is the difference between sales and purchases: the net cash flow from real economic activity. The second is the difference between dividends paid to shareholders and issues of new shares.

The former may be described as the corporate cash flow base and the latter as the net equity distributions base. To see the relationship between the two examine the corporate sources and uses of funds shown in Table B.1. In terms of the notation of Table B.1, the two tax bases, denoted by TB_1 and TB_2 respectively, are given by the equations:

$$TB_1 = R - I \tag{1}$$

$$TB_2 = D - S \tag{2}$$

From the flow of funds identity it follows that

$$TB_2 + T = TB_1 + (B - P)$$

The differences between the corporate cash flow and net equity distributions bases can be seen to be the following. First, because taxes paid enter into

TABLE B.1   Corporate sources and uses of funds

Sources	Uses
R Receipts from sales of goods and services less purchases of labour, raw materials, and services	*I* Investment expenditure (gross investment less receipts from sales of assets)
B Borrowing (new issues of debt less repayment of old debt)	*P* Interest payments (net of interest received)
S New share issues (less share repurchases), including net sales of shares in other companies	*D* Dividends paid (less dividends received)
	T Taxes paid

Accounting identity: $R + B + S = I + P + D + T$

the sources and uses of funds statement, the corporate cash flow basis is a measure of the tax base on a tax-inclusive basis, whereas the definition in terms of net equity distributions is measured on a tax-exclusive basis. If the tax rate on the corporate cash flow base were 50 per cent, then this would be equivalent to a tax rate of 100 per cent on the net equity distribution base. Secondly, to the extent that a company earns real profits from transactions in financial assets (other than equities), then the corporate cash flow base would not include those profits. Only if the net equity distributions base were used would such profits be taxed. This is a major consideration for financial institutions, such as banks, which derive their earnings primarily from the provision of financial services for which no direct charge is levied but which are reflected in differences between borrowing and lending rates. The same phenomenon can be observed in the national accounts, in which the real economic profits of the financial sector are recorded as negative. This is because the national accounts use real transactions to measure profits and ignore profits on financial transactions. If no profit is made on such financial transactions, then the present value of interest payments equals the present value of net borrowing, and over time, and given a constant tax rate, the corporate cash flow base and the equity distributions base are identical. This is likely to be approximately true for major industrial corporations, and as far as non-financial activity is concerned the two bases have identical economic effects. The two bases could be made identically equal by modifying the corporate cash flow base to include the difference between net new borrowing and net interest payments. In other words, interest deductibility would continue, but new borrowing would constitute a taxable receipt.

1. Problems of implementation

1.1 Transitional arrangements

Two sets of issues arise in the design of transitional arrangements. The first consists of the problems that arise from the application of the new tax base. The second is the question of how far the expected consequences of the old base are continued after the introduction of the new tax. The second is the easier to deal with and so is considered first.

On the date when the new base comes into force, companies have a stock of depreciation allowances that they expect to be able to carry forward and deduct (in a pre-determined time profile) against future taxable profits. There seems no good reason to deny companies the right to continue to deduct depreciation allowances on past investment. To abolish the existing stock of depreciation allowances would be akin to a windfall profits tax in proportion to past investment: not a happy precedent to set. Moreover, unless the date on which the tax becomes effective can be made retrospective, anticipation of the change would lead to a collapse in investment in the period between announcement and the date when the enabling legislation was passed.

Similar arguments apply to other forms of 'losses' that companies had expected to be able to carry forward to offset against future profits. Continuation of such loss carry forwards is straightforward under the real basis, but with the net dividends basis the simplicity of the tax would be reduced because net distributions constitute a tax-exclusive base whereas loss carry forwards are inherited from a tax-inclusive regime. To retain simplicity, the loss carry forwards could be converted into a stock of tax credits (or, more generally, a flow of tax credits over time) on the transition date.

The other set of problems results from the implications of the new base although their nature differs as between the real and net distributions bases. With the former, the main problem is that debt interest payments are no longer tax-deductible. For new debt finance this raises no problems, but for borrowing incurred before the announcement of the new base there is a retrospective charge on the cost of servicing the debt which in some, perhaps many, cases could cause acute financial distress for highly geared companies. One solution is simply to phase out interest deductibility by reducing the proportion of interest payments that are deductible gradually—over a period of, say, five to ten years—from unity to zero. As far as the net distributions basis is concerned, there is a more serious transitional problem. Unless the new basis became effective on the date of announcement, companies would have a strong incentive to raise their debt–equity ratios by borrowing and paying high dividends before the transition date, and then to issue new equity in order to repay the loans and reduce dividends after the transition date in order to repay the loans and restore their debt–equity ratios to normal levels. Similar incentives existed in the UK during the major corporate tax reforms of 1965 and 1973, and although revenue losses occurred, the problem was regarded as manageable. Nevertheless, anti-avoidance provisions would be necessary because the scope for avoidance using purely financial transactions is large.

1.2 Long-run administrative problems

In this section we describe some of the administrative problems that the tax would present on a permanent basis. The first concerns the treatment of borrowing. Under the corporate cash flow basis, only real transactions are taken into account; profits made on financial transactions are exempt from tax. This does not appear to be a satisfactory method of taxing financial institutions. If the cash flow base were adopted then a separate tax would be required for such institutions. Alternatively, under the net equity distributions basis, which does tax the profits on financial transactions, rules would be required to prevent companies from issuing debt at artificially high interest rates. Such payments would be exempt from corporate tax and would be a method of returning profits to the shareholders free of tax. Of course, this problem exists under the current tax with interest deductibility. Current rules would need to be carried over. Some of the other problems that exist with the current corporate tax system would remain with the new tax. There would still need to be a distinction between corporate and personal expenditure in order to levy the appropriate amounts of personal income tax on benefits provided by the company. Under the net equity distributions basis, new rules would be required to determine the amount of dividends that enter the tax base when some part of the dividend was paid in kind. Shareholder benefits of all types (for example, reductions in the price of the company's products when sold to its shareholders) come under this heading.

A second area of potential problems concerns the phenomenon of tax exhaustion. This is the situation in which the company has no current taxable income and is accumulating tax losses that will be carried forward. A question that arises is how far it is thought to be acceptable for companies to trade such tax losses among themselves. Under the existing tax systems in both the US and the UK, trading of tax losses takes place with leasing. The US authorities have taken a much harder line on this than their UK counterparts, although it is not easy to see why companies should be prevented from offsetting the unintended effects of an asymmetric tax system. The limiting case would be to create a market in corporate tax losses. Failing that, companies could be allowed to carry forward losses marked up by the market interest rate which would leave the incentive to invest unaffected by the asymmetric treatment of positive and negative taxable profits. In the absence of such a provision, leasing would be the market solution under the corporate cash flow basis. Under the net equity distributions basis, a rather different set of companies would be tax exhausted. These would be firms that had made substantial issues of new shares. Such a company could reduce its tax loss by borrowing in order to purchase shares in other resident companies, and in the absence of loss carry forward with interest would have an incentive to do so.

Although these problems are rather different under the two alternative bases, they do not seem to be more serious under one than the other. The cash flow basis perhaps has a cosmetic advantage in appearing more familiar. But the net equity distributions basis would enable the revenue authorities to adopt a common fiscal year for all companies without the need for companies to change their own accounting periods.

The treatment of overseas investment and profits remitted from abroad also raises some important questions. With a cash flow corporation tax there is no obvious reason to grant credit for foreign taxes paid. This is because the government is a partner in the firm's equity. If the foreign corporate tax rate is at least as great as the domestic tax rate, then the government would receive no return on its investment in the firm's activities overseas. But if foreign tax credit is denied then the firm receives a return on its own share of the investment equal to the net of foreign tax rate return on the investment, i.e. the return to society on this investment overseas. One problem with the denial of foreign tax credit is that it would be difficult to impute that part of foreign taxes attributable to investment made after the introduction of the cash flow tax and that part attributable to investment made before the change in the system. Hence an alternative means of achieving the same objective would be to deny investment relief for overseas investment. Under the cash flow base this would be straightforward in that the investment made overseas would not qualify for immediate expensing. With the net equity distributions base, an additional tax would be levied on overseas investment at the appropriate tax-inclusive rate. When the foreign tax rate was below the domestic corporate tax rate, then the additional charge (or reduction in allowances for investment) would be scaled down in proportion to the ratio of the two tax rates. It is interesting to note that for twelve years (1972–84), the UK government did allow companies both to receive 100 per cent first year allowances on overseas investment made by branches and also to receive credit for foreign taxes paid. This was effectively a subsidy to overseas investment. Nevertheless, it seems unlikely that this position would be maintained if there were a permanent shift to a cash flow corporation tax.

C

Schemas for Macroeconomic Policy Co-ordination

There is a strong intuitive belief among many policy-makers, which is supported by a rapidly expanding literature of theoretical and applied analysis [1], that co-operation in macroeconomic policy among highly interdependent economies that retain institutional independence in the conduct of policy will deliver superior outcomes to a non-cooperative regime. However, co-operation cannot function without some underlying standard, which may be explicit or implicit. The automatic adjustment mechanisms of the gold standard has been mentioned, and only because of them did this system last for some time.[1] The Bretton Woods system was successful while the dollar provided a satisfactory standard. The European Monetary System has made good use of an implicit Deutschmark standard during its period of disinflation.

For reasons that have already been indicated (in section 12.1), there is now a need to identify a more general and symmetrical standard for macroeconomic policy co-ordination in the Community, as indeed also in the wider grouping of industrialized countries. Within the Community, and the European Monetary System in particular, this search for a standard will in any case be prompted by technical factors. As already indicated above, when capital markets are liberalized, reliance on a single country's monetary policy as the pivot of the system would not be satisfactory. The 'divergence indicator' of the EMS was inspired by the need for a symmetrical standard but has not proved effective. According to this indicator, where a currency moves beyond 75 per cent of its maximum permissible fluctuation margins in relation to the ECU, the authorities of that country are subject to the presumption that they should make a policy adjustment. The ineffectiveness of the 'divergence indicator' was partly for technical reasons, because not all currencies in the ECU participate in the exchange rate mechanism of the EMS.

The reduction of inflation, but persistence of unemployment, is a further and more fundamental reason why the lack of symmetry in the present *ad hoc* system of co-ordination becomes an issue of increasing practical importance. The rigours of completing the internal market add to the need for a sufficiently positive growth environment in Europe, and this concern is expressed in the Single European Act under the requirements of 'cohesion'

---

[1] While recognizing these qualities of the gold standard, the Group does not consider this system an option to be considered because of the arbitrariness of the gold supply.

(Art. 130). The search for an agreed standard to help guide the co-ordination process is thus desirable. Indeed, a system of co-ordination, if it is to go beyond *ad hoc* episodes of occasionally linked policy moves, requires a standard. If gold is not acceptable, and individual key currencies not permanently so, then macroeconomic indicators have to supply the standard.

A variety of academic proposals for co-ordination standards have emerged in recent years, and the search for practical solutions has also been encouraged by the support given at the 1986 Tokyo Summit of the seven largest industrialized countries for an indicator system to help guide economic policy co-ordination. By way of example, a recent paper by Williamson [2] has set out, within a unified framework, four alternative 'standards' which could in principle be used as a presumptive indicator of how policy adjustments should be made. The key idea is to identify criteria which, in the event of exchange rate tensions within a system of pegged exchange rates, would indicate (*a*) how the burden of policy adjustment should be distributed between appreciating or depreciating currency countries and (*b*) whether monetary or budgetary policy instruments would be used. The standards are as follows:

1. *A business conjuncture standard.* The level of real economic activity in the group of economies would be the primary indicator. Where the business conjuncture was strong, the weak currency countries would raise interest rates; where the conjuncture was weak, the strong currency countries would reduce them.

2. *An inflation standard.* The rate of inflation would be the primary indicator. This could be the average rate for the group of countries, or, alternatively, the rate of increase for a basket of world commodity prices. When the rate of inflation was high, the weak currency countries would raise interest rates; and vice versa when the rate of inflation was very low.

3. *A money supply standard.* The rate of increase in money supply for the group of countries would be the primary indicator. This corresponds to the idea advocated by McKinnon [3], which allows for shifts in portfolios of different currencies without destabilizing the international economy. Where the aggregate money supply of the group was above target, the weak currency countries would raise interest rates; and vice versa when money supply was below target.

4. *A nominal income standard.* This is analogous to the preceding standard, except that it would disregard unexpected changes in velocity of monetary circulation (e.g. because of financial innovations). The evolution of nominal income (or nominal GDP) of the group would be the primary indicator. When the group's nominal income was above the programmed level, the weak currency countries would raise interest rates; and vice versa when the nominal income was growing weakly.

These standards have the following strengths and weaknesses. The first two standards can be criticized for privileging only one of the main objectives of economic policy. The money supply standard is vulnerable to unpredictable

TABLE C.1   A possible schema for macroeconomic policy co-ordination: presumptive policy reactions to deviations of indicators from target

Macroeconomic evolution of the group of countries	Exchange rate of individual countries	
	Appreciating above group margins	Depreciating below group margins
Above standard	Monetary expansion, fiscal contraction	Monetary contraction
Below standard	Monetary expansion	Monetary contraction, fiscal expansion

Source: Adapted from Williamson [2].
Note: The macroeconomic evolution could be identified, in principle, in terms of any of the four standards described in the text—the business conjuncture, inflation, money supply, or nominal income.

behaviour of monetary velocity. The nominal income standard avoids this problem and is a plausible compromise between the first two standards, although there are still difficulties of prompt and accurate information and control over the evolution of this variable.

Each of these indicators could in principle be related to a general schema for indicating where the presumption to make policy adjustments lay. This schema (as indicated in Table C.1) would guide the distribution of macroeconomic policy adjustments between countries in the event of exchange rate tensions. *Monetary policy would be the first and primary policy to adjust. Fiscal policy would have more room for decentralized management.* However, there would be circumstances when supporting fiscal policy adjustments would be indicated.

It will not be easy to reach agreement over the choice of standard, nor over the strength of the presumption to act in accordance with the indicators. In particular, it is not conceivable that a wholly automatic system of 'rules' will come to exclude any significant role for 'discretion'. None the less, the standards set out above encompass a range of possibilities, or at least a framework of ideas, within which the search for a balanced standard for presumptive policy reactions may be pursued.

References

[1] W. Buiter and R. Marston, *International Economic Policy Co-ordination*. Cambridge University Press, 1985.
[2] J. Williamson, *Options for Improving the International Co-ordination of Economic Policies*. Marcus Wallenberg Papers on International Finance, International Law Institute, Georgetown University, Washington DC, 1987.
[3] R. McKinnon, *An International Standard for Monetary Stabilization*. International Institute for Economics, 1984.

D

Distributive Aspects of the Community Budget

---

1. Basic data

The basic data for discussing these budgetary issues consist of:

1. Income per capita by country and region.
2. Budgetary own resources and contributions.
3. Budgetary expenditures.

1.1. Income per capita

The basic standard for questions of fiscal equity within the Community is GDP per capita. Two sets of figures are needed: first, the data converted at market exchange rates, since actual financial transactions and tax collections relate to these figures; secondly, data converted onto a purchasing power parity (PPP) basis. In the second case, harmonized surveys of prices are conducted by the Statistical Office of the EC, producing indices which allow national accounts aggregates, such as GDP, to be converted to a comparable basis from the point of view of living standards. The latter data are more suitable parameters for use in relation to scales of fiscal progressivity between countries, or needs for regional assistance (see Table I).

1.2. Budgetary own resources and contributions

A recent Communication by the Commission [1] has given a breakdown by country of the present budgetary resources, with data estimated for 1987. For the new Member States the data are 'theoretical' estimates, in the sense that they suppose that the transitional arrangements presently limiting these countries' budgetary contributions were no longer in operation (see Table II).

In the current Fontainebleau mechanism (see Ch. 13, n. 4) it is supposed, for the purpose of calculation, that VAT accounts for all financing of the budget. This allows customs duties to be excluded from the calculation, on the grounds that the point of collection for these taxes may be a poor guide to their incidence. Similar procedures could, if desired, be built into the safeguard mechanism presented below.

The Commission's recent proposals [1] include an additional budgetary resource, which would be a contribution key related to Gross National Product (GNP, which is not much different from GDP). This marginal source of finance would be calculated such that the total of the VAT revenues and the marginal amount would conform to a GNP distribution key. Thus, the new element would correct for deviations of VAT revenues from a GNP standard, as well as adding some further revenues beyond the present VAT ceiling. These Commission proposals are equivalent to what the report called a 'neutral' marginal financing of the budget (i.e. neutral with respect to GNP at market prices).

1.3. Budgetary expenditures

For the purpose of the simulation exercises presented below, expenditures from the budget have been grouped, and distributed by country, as follows:

1. *Agricultural expenditure.* The country breakdown given in the Commission source (see Table III) for 1986 is assumed to remain constant in percentage terms for all the 1992 scenarios presented below.

2. *Structural funds.* These are distributed by country according to the key given in Table III. This assumes equal per capita receipts for the populations covered by the eligibility criteria of the funds. Simplified assumptions for this purpose are given in the footnotes to Table III. No official estimates are available for the future distribution of the total amount of structural funds. The assumptions made here for the purposes of budgetary sensitivity analysis do *not* imply a policy recommendation on the part of the Group.

3. *Other policies (allocated).* This category covers policies whose expenditure can in principle be allocated by country. Since the policies concerned do not have particular regional or distributive objectives, it is assumed that they are distributed on a *pro rata* GDP basis. The outcome might be otherwise, but there are not sufficient grounds for an alternative working hypothesis.

4. *Other expenditures (unallocated).* This covers either policy expenditures which cannot be allocated by country (such as external expenditures on development aid), or Community administrative expenditures which represent a Community 'public good'. It could be justifiable to attribute some percentages of administrative expenditures to the countries of location of Community institutions, but this has not been done.

2. Budget scenarios

The six scenarios (detailed in Panel 13.1 in the report and Table IV) are based on the following elements.

1. All scenarios relate to 1992, with money amounts in 1992 prices.

2. GDP of the Community grows annually from 1987 to 1992, by 6 per cent in nominal terms (3.5 per cent in volume and 2.5 per cent in inflation).

3. The budget total is constrained to a constant share of GDP (1.1 per cent). The actual budget outcome for 1987, the basis of the simulation below, is at present uncertain. The budget adopted by the Council in February 1987 totalled 37 billion ECUs, but it is widely recognized that this understated certain expenditures, including agriculture. Commission projections [1] point to a possible outcome of 42 billion ECUs. The simulations therefore assume a

Annexes

rounded 1987 baseline figure of 40 billion ECUs, with 24 billion ECUs of
agricultural expenditure, and 6 billion ECUs for the structural funds.

4. Agricultural expenditure then remains constant either in GDP share
(scenarios 1 and 4), or in real terms (scenarios 2 and 5), or in nominal terms
(3 and 6).

5. The structural funds and other policies (allocated) then grow at different
speeds, within the constraints of the budget total and the agricultural
scenarios.

6. Other expenditures (unallocated) are assumed to remain at a constant
nominal amount of 7 billion ECUs. However, the 1987 amount includes
refunds to Member States (VAT refunds, UK Fontainebleau mechanism)
which is not included in the 1992 scenarios (the VAT refunds are assumed to
be discontinued, and rebates under the Safeguard Mechanism are assumed to
be accounted for on the revenue side of the budget). Therefore there is room at
least for a constant real level of expenditure on Community administrative
and other expenditures.

7. The marginal financing of the budget is assumed to be either 'neutral'
with respect to GDP (scenarios 1, 2 and 3) or 'progressive' with respect to
GDP (scenarios 4, 5 and 6). The specific values for these two keys are given in
Table V. The 'progressive' marginal financing source could to some extent be
superfluous, depending upon the progressively characteristics of the safeguard
mechanism set out below.

The basic budget data for the simulations may be summarized as shown in
Table D.I.

3. A safeguard mechanism in broad outline

The objective of the safeguard mechanism would be to assure a broad range of
budgetary outcomes by country, such that a certain standard of progressive
fiscal equity were assured. A broad range of outcomes, rather than precisely
targeted outcomes, would be the objective, so that the policies of the
Community would have 'room' to pursue their specific policy objectives, often

TABLE D.1   Basic budget data for the simulations (billions of ECU at current 1987 or
1992 prices)

	1987	Scenarios for 1992		
		1 and 4	2 and 5	3 and 6
Agriculture	24	32	27	24
Structural funds	6	10	14	16
Other policies (allocated)	3	5	6	7
Other expenditure (unallocated)	7	7	7	7
TOTAL	40	54	54	54

of a sectoral nature. To constrain the budget outcomes tightly would mean destroying the incentive mechanisms of individual policies (for example, if an extra effort by a country's authorities to organize an R&D project eligible for Community financing were offset by a corrective payment to keep that country's net transfer position unchanged).

The safeguard mechanism could operate in relation either to (*a*) the net transfer position of individual countries or (*b*) the expenditure side of the budget alone. In both cases, a *normative curve* would be established (in a formula, of which possible examples are described below), in which the poorest countries would be the recipient of the largest net transfers (or expenditures) and in which the richest countries would be the payers of the largest net transfers (or recipients of the smallest amounts of expenditures), all amounts being expressed in percentage shares of GDP. The curve would assure progressivity in this distribution system, but as income increased, progressivity would become less and less steep.

Around the normative curve, there would be *bands*, within which the outcome would be freely determined by individual policies. As explained in the main text, outcomes above the bands (i.e. relatively unfavourable to the country concerned) would give rise to a corrective payment from the budget to that country. Outcomes below the bands (i.e. relatively favourable) would give rise *either* to corrective payments from the country to the budget *or*, in the case only of low-income countries, to the need for associated agreement with the Community over medium-term macroeconomic policy conditions. These conditions would aim at convergence on monetary stability, or a sustainable public debt situation, for example.

The precise slope and shape of the curve and the bands could only be determined in the course of political negotiation. However, the formula set out in the next section has the quality that these negotiations could turn around the values to be given to just two or three parameters.

4. A formula for a safeguard mechanism

4.1. Basic method

The method proposed defines the relation between the rate of net contribution of a country (expressed as a percentage of GDP) and its income per capita. The rate of the net contribution is a rising function, at a declining rate, of income per capita.

The net contribution of country i, N_i, is:

$$N_i = (\lambda_i - \rho) \, Y_i \tag{1}$$

where Y_i is the GDP of country i, λ_i is a coefficient measuring the contributive capacity of country i, and ρ is a coefficient measuring the average contributive capacity.

Coefficient ρ is defined so that the sum of net contributions is sufficient to finance non-allocated Community expenditure (such as administrative expenditures, development aid, etc.) Thus

$$\rho = \frac{\sum_i \lambda_i Y_i - B}{\sum_i Y_i} \tag{2}$$

where B is non-allocated Community expenditures, and ρ is such that

$$\sum_i N_i = B$$

From (1), it is established that Country i is a net contributor if $\lambda_i > \rho$, and Country i is a net recipient if $\lambda_i < \rho$. The contributive capacity of a country i, λ_i, is a monotonically increasing function of its income per capita:

$$\lambda_i = \ln(y_i^\beta) \tag{3}$$

where y_i is income per capita of country i (measured in terms of purchasing power parity).

The coefficient β describes the change in contributive capacity for a given relative variation in income per capita:

$$\beta = \frac{d\lambda_i}{\dfrac{dy_i}{y_i}} \tag{4}$$

The higher this coefficient, the greater is the transfer of resources between rich and poor countries. The coefficient is therefore an indicator of the desired redistributive effect.

The elasticity of λ_i in relation to y_i, μ, is:

$$\mu = \frac{\beta}{\lambda_i} = \frac{1}{\ln y_i} \tag{5}$$

This elasticity declines as a function of income per head. In other words, a variation of 1 per cent in income per head has a weaker impact on the contributive capacity of a country when that country's income per capita — and therefore its contributive capacity — is high.

Substituting (3) and (2) into (1), and assuming non-allocated Community expenditures to be nil ($B = 0$), one has:

$$\frac{N_i}{Y_i} = \sum_j \frac{\beta Y_j}{\sum_j Y_j} \ln \frac{y_i}{y_j} \tag{6}$$

Putting $\dfrac{Y_j}{\sum_j Y_j} = a_j$, (6) becomes:

$$\frac{N_i}{Y_i} = \beta \ln \frac{y_i}{\prod_j y_j^{a_j}} \tag{7}$$

where $\prod_j y_j^{a_j}$ is a geometric average of income per head weighted by the share of GDP of each country in the Community's total GDP (a_j).

We have:

$$\frac{N_i}{Y_i} > 0 \text{ if } \ln \frac{y_i}{\prod_j y_j^{a_j}} > 0, \text{ and therefore if } \frac{y_i}{\prod_j y_j^{a_j}} > 1$$

$$\frac{N_i}{Y_i} < 0 \text{ if } \ln \frac{y_i}{\prod_j y_j^{a_j}} < 0, \text{ and therefore if } \frac{y_i}{\prod_j y_j^{a_j}} < 1$$

According to (7), a country i is a net recipient of resources if its income per head y_i is inferior to the weighted average income per head in the Community $\prod_j y_j^{a_j}$.

4.2. *Method of calculation of the safeguard mechanism*

Formula (1) can be written:

$$\frac{N_i}{Y_i} = \ln (y_i^\beta) - \rho \tag{8}$$

Bands about this curve are obtained by setting a constant distance on the horizontal axis to the right and left of the central curve, thus:

$$\frac{N_i}{Y_i} = \ln (y_i^\beta \pm \varepsilon) - \rho \tag{9}$$

where ε is the value of the horizontal distance. Fig. D.1 illustrates this:

FIG. D.1   Curve and bands of a safeguard mechanism

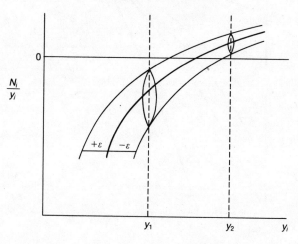

The acceptable limits of net transfers ($\mathcal{N}_i/\Upsilon_i$) are greater when income per capita (y_i) is lower, and vice versa. In this way, it would be possible to vary the net contribution more for net beneficiaries, which could permit increasing room for quality control conditions to be associated with resource transfers where these become relatively important as a share of the beneficiary's GDP.

4.3. Options

The curve linking net contributions to income per head can be modulated as a function of:

1. Parameter β, according to whether a more or less pronounced redistributive effect is desired. Fig. D. 2 gives examples for $\beta = 0.1, 0.05, 0.04, 0.03$, and 0.01.

2. The relationship between contributive capacity and income per head. For example, instead of $\lambda_i = \ln y_i$, one could have $\ln \lambda_i = \ln y_i$.

3. Parameter ε, which determines the width of the safeguard mechanism.

Finally, it is also possible that the safeguard mechanism relates only to expenditure, rather than to net transfers. Fig. D.3 illustrates how this curve would compare to that for net transfers.

FIG. D.2   Alternative curves for the safeguard mechanism

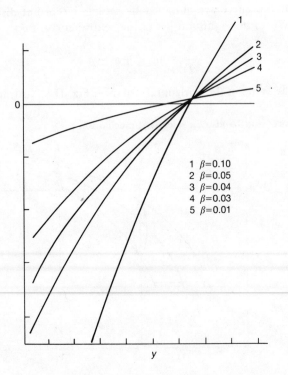

1 $\beta=0.10$
2 $\beta=0.05$
3 $\beta=0.04$
4 $\beta=0.03$
5 $\beta=0.01$

y

FIG. D.3   Net balance and expenditure mechanisms

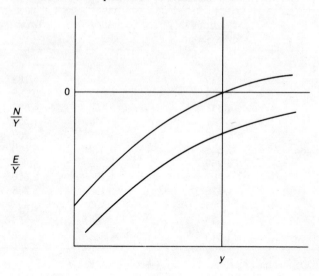

TABLE I   Gross domestic product per capita in the EC in 1985

	At current market exchange rates		At PPP exchange rates[a]
	ECU	Index	Index
Luxemburg	14,175	133.5	129.3
Denmark	16,166	152.5	123.9
Germany	14,785	139.2	121.6
France	12,934	121.8	114.0
Belgium	11,443	107.8	109.8
Netherlands	11,842	111.5	106.1
United Kingdom	10,333	97.3	102.0
Italy	9,052	85.3	91.7
Spain	6,135	57.8	75.0
Ireland	7,583	71.4	70.4
Greece	3,847	36.2	57.1
Portugal	2,860	26.9	46.2
EC-12	10,618	100	100

Source: Commision of the European Communities, *European Economy* no. 30 Nov. 1986.
[a]PPP = purchasing power parity.

TABLE II   Financing of the Community budget, 1987 (million ECUs)

	Traditional own resources	VAT	Total
Luxemburg	5	63	68
Denmark	255	528	783
Germany	2,808	6,878	9,686
France	1,333	5,158	6,692
Belgium	784	770	1,554
Netherlands	976	1,233	2,209
United Kingdom	2,338	4,322	6,660
Italy	1,259	3,546	4,806
Spain	1,107	1,704	2,810
Ireland	170	196	366
Greece	123	300	423
Portugal	158	186	344
EC-12	11,515	24,865	36,400

Source: Commission of the EC, *Future Financing of the Community Budget*, COM (87) 101, February 1987.

TABLE III   Hypothesis for the allocation of Community budget expenditures by country (percentages)

	Agriculture[a]	Structural funds[b]	Other policies (allocated)[c]
Luxemburg	0.01	—	0.2
Denmark	3.95	—	2.4
Germany	18.73	—	26.3
France	23.54	11.9	20.9
Belgium	4.78	2.1	3.3
Netherlands	9.32	1.6	5.0
United Kingdom	9.65	17.8	17.0
Italy	14.05	21.0	15.1
Spain	4.79	20.7	7.0
Ireland	5.20	3.7	0.8
Greece	5.58	10.6	1.1
Portugal	0.39	10.7	0.9
EC-12	100.0	100.0	100.0

[a]Actual figures for 1986. Source: Commission of the EC. *Future Financing of the Community Budget*, COM (87) 101 Feburary 1987.
[b]The structural funds are hypothetically distributed on the basis that the regions eligible account for the following percentages of the population: Portugal 100%, Greece 100%, Ireland 100%, Spain 50%, Italy 35%, United Kingdom 30%, Belgium 20%, France 20%, Netherlands 10%. Sums received are then equal pro rata capita.
[c]Allocated hypothetically pro rata GDP.

TABLE IV Simulations of scenarios for the Community budget in 1992 (percentages of GDP)

Item	Scenario 1 Constant GDP share / Small increase / Neutral			Scenario 2 Constant real / Medium increase / Neutral			Scenario 3 Constant nominal / Large increase / Neutral		
Agricultural expenditure / Structural/other expenditure / Financing	Expenditure	Financing	Balance	Expenditure	Financing	Balance	Expenditure	Financing	Balance
Luxemburg	0.30	1.69	-1.39	0.37	1.69	-1.32	0.40	1.69	-1.29
Denmark	1.61	1.50	0.12	1.44	1.50	-0.05	1.34	1.50	-0.16
Germany	0.82	1.50	-0.68	0.78	1.50	-0.72	0.75	1.50	-0.75
France	1.39	1.42	-0.03	1.35	1.42	-0.08	1.32	1.42	-0.11
Belgium	1.70	1.92	-0.21	1.61	1.92	-0.31	1.55	1.92	-0.37
Netherlands	1.97	1.80	0.18	1.79	1.80	-0.01	1.68	1.80	-0.12
United Kingdom	1.03	1.51	-0.48	1.09	1.51	-0.42	1.13	1.51	-0.38
Italy	1.40	1.38	0.02	1.44	1.38	0.06	1.46	1.38	0.09
Spain	1.67	1.49	0.18	1.86	1.49	0.37	1.99	1.49	0.50
Ireland	7.42	1.66	5.76	6.95	1.66	5.30	6.70	1.66	5.04
Greece	7.67	1.50	6.17	7.80	1.50	6.30	7.93	1.50	6.42
Portugal	4.48	1.67	2.80	5.52	1.67	3.85	6.21	1.67	4.54
EC-12	—	—	—	—	—	—	—	—	—

TABLE IV (continued)

Item	Scenario 4 Constant GDP share Small increase Progressive			Scenario 5 Constant real Medium increase Progressive			Scenario 6 Constant nominal Large increase Progressive		
Agricultural expenditure Structural/other expenditure Financing	Expenditure	Financing	Balance	Expenditure	Financing	Balance	Expenditure	Financing	Balance
Luxemburg	0.30	1.84	−1.54	0.37	1.84	−1.48	0.40	1.84	−1.44
Denmark	1.61	1.60	0.01	1.44	1.60	−0.15	1.34	1.60	−0.26
Germany	0.82	1.59	−0.76	0.78	1.59	−0.81	0.75	1.59	−0.84
France	1.39	1.47	−0.08	1.35	1.47	−0.12	1.32	1.47	−0.15
Belgium	1.70	1.94	−0.24	1.61	1.94	−0.33	1.55	1.94	−0.39
Netherlands	1.97	1.80	0.18	1.79	1.80	−0.01	1.68	1.80	−0.12
United Kingdom	1.03	1.49	−0.46	1.09	1.49	−0.40	1.13	1.49	−0.36
Italy	1.40	1.30	0.10	1.44	1.30	0.14	1.46	1.30	0.17
Spain	1.67	1.31	0.36	1.86	1.31	0.55	1.99	1.31	0.68
Ireland	7.42	1.45	5.96	6.95	1.45	5.50	6.70	1.45	5.25
Greece	7.67	1.22	6.45	7.80	1.22	6.58	7.93	1.22	6.70
Portugal	4.48	1.31	3.17	5.52	1.31	4.21	6.21	1.31	4.90
EC-12	–	–	–	–	–	–	–	–	–

Notes: Countries are rank-ordered by GDP per capita. For details on methods and assumptions, see text.

TABLE V Financing keys for the budget 'neutral' and 'progressive' with respect to GDP

	GDP per capita at PPP (index)	GDP % share at market exchange rates	GDP % share corrected with progressivity coefficient[a]
	(1)	(2)	(3)
Luxemburg	129.3	0.2	0.2
Denmark	123.9	2.4	2.6
Germany	121.6	26.3	28.3
France	114.0	20.9	21.7
Belgium	109.8	3.3	3.4
Netherlands	106.1	5.0	5.1
United Kingdom	102.0	17.0	16.7
Italy	91.7	15.1	14.0
Spain	75.0	7.0	5.9
Ireland	70.7	0.8	0.7
Greece	57.1	1.1	0.8
Portugal	46.2	0.9	0.6
EC-12	100.0	100.0	100.0

[a] $Y_i^c = \dfrac{Y_i \times C_i}{\sum_i Y_i \times C_i} \times 100$ where:

Y_i^c = corrected GDP share of country i (col. 3)
Y_i = non-corrected GDP share of country i (col. 2)
C_i = correction coefficient of country i
$C_i = \dfrac{I_i - 100}{2} + 100$
I_i = GDP per capita index of country i (col. 1)

E

The Less-favoured Regions of the Community

This annex briefly explains the size and importance of regional disparities in the Community and gives rough estimates of the amount of physical and human capital formation that might accompany an improvement of the economic performance of the less-favoured regions.

1. Regional disparities

Regional disparities within the Community are important, much more than in the United States for instance. Moreover, the successive enlargements of the Community have substantially increased its regional problems: the accession of Greece (1981) and of Spain and Portugal (1986) has increased GDP by 10 per cent, population by 22 per cent, and employment in agriculture by 57 per cent. The population living in regions whose GDP per capita in purchasing power parity terms (PPP) is 25 per cent below the Community average has risen from 24 million (i.e. just under 10 per cent) to 62 million (i.e. 20 per cent of the enlarged Community population).

The ratio of GDP per capita in PPP is 1 to 5 between Thrace in Greece and Hamburg in Germany. The unemployment rate varies from 3 per cent in Luxemburg to 30 per cent in Andalucia in Spain. The endowment in basic economic infrastructure shows a ratio of 1 to 12 between Thrace and Hamburg. The regions with low income, deficient infrastructure endowment, and (generally) high unemployment have mostly also a high share of employment in agriculture (more than 25 per cent). Maps I–III at the end of this annex give a comprehensive picture of regional disparities in the enlarged Community.

The evolution of these aggregates has been rather complex. In the 1960s there was relative convergence in real GDP per capita between countries, but since the first energy crisis in 1973, this trend seems to have come to a stop and the gaps have been stabilized or slightly increased (Fig. E.1). The unemployment rate in the Community has grown from 2 per cent at the beginning of the 1970s to nearly 11 per cent in 1986, with a growing regional divergence (Fig. E.2). As far as infrastructure endowment is concerned, a certain effort has been made in the last decade to close the gap.

The problem regions in the Community can be classified in two categories (see Table E.5 at the end of this annex). The first is composed of the *least-favoured regions*. They are characterized by a deficient basic infrastructure and low productivity. In most cases they are located at the Community's

Fig. E.1   GDP inequalities between Member States: standard deviation of real GDP per capita as a ratio of the Community average in percentage terms

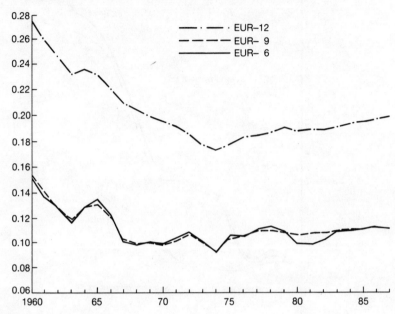

Source: European Commission.

periphery. Their income per capita is very low (less than 75 per cent of the Community average), and the share of total income from a low-productivity agricultural sector is relatively large. They often are or have been zones of heavy emigration. Demographic expansion is still considerable (1 per cent per annum). They represent about 20 per cent of the Community's population. These regions include Portugal, Greece, Ireland, the south of Italy, and about half of Spain (centre–south–west), to which may be added Northern Ireland and the French overseas departments.

The category of *declining industrial regions* is more difficult to define. Their formerly flourishing economy has been weakened by structural change in industry at the European or even world level. Regions with heavy concentrations of mining, steel, textile, or ship-building industries are in need of reconversion and professional educational programmes more than infrastructure equipment, which is generally relatively satisfactory. They also generally show a high level of unemployment. As a first approach, one might identify this category in terms of those regions whose GDP per capita is between 75 and 100 per cent of the Community average, whose unemployment rate is above the Community average (10.8 per cent in 1986), and whose territories

FIG. E.2 Trend of unemployment in the Community

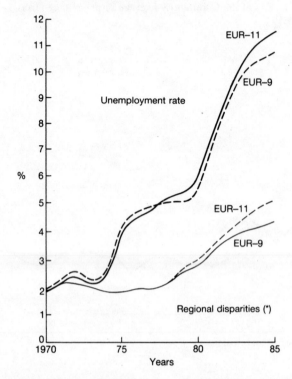

Source: European Commission, *Third Periodic Report on the Social and Economic Situation and Development of the Regions of the European Community* (forthcoming).
Note: Indications based on the statistics for the registered unemployed. Greece could not be included since its unemployment statistics do not lend themselves to this type of analysis.
(*) Standard deviation weighted by the regional shares of the labour force.

are, wholly or partially, designated for national regional aid schemes. In contrast to the first category, their geographical distribution can change rapidly. According to these criteria, about 10 per cent of the Community's population lived in such areas. They are mainly situated in the north and west of the United Kingdom, the north and east of France, in the north of Spain and the east of Belgium and of the Netherlands. According to this definition, there would be no such regions in Denmark, Germany, or Luxemburg. However, these rough criteria are insufficient to identify at all precisely or surely the category of declining industrial regions, and the report therefore does not pretend to draw up a list of regions of direct operational use for the Community's regional policies.

2. Quantitative perspectives on regional capital formation

In order to induce convergence of productivity and living standards in the Community, the less-favoured countries and regions of the Community (i.e. both above-mentioned categories) will have to achieve a higher growth rate than the Community average over a long period, as happened in the 1960s.

In order to obtain some illustrative orders of magnitude of the amount of investment required to make possible an additional one percentage point growth in GDP in these regions, a simple growth model is supposed (see panel).

Statistical data on marginal efficiency of investment have been estimated on the basis of average growth rates of real GDP and ratios of net investment to GDP over different periods. The marginal efficiency of investment (MEI) is rather unstable in time (for the Community as a whole it varies from 0.19 to 0.33).

The MEIs are only available at the country level. In the case of Portugal, Greece, and Ireland this raises no problem since these countries are considered as less favoured in their totality. For other countries estimates were made according to two methods:

Method 1: the MEI in the regions considered is the same as in the country taken as a whole.

Method 2: the MEI in the regions considered is lower than in the country taken as a whole.[1]

The estimated trend values of MEI—taking into account their evolution over time—are given in Table E.1. Countries are ranked by GDP per capita. All country (and regional) values are below the estimated Community trend value of 0.27, with the exception of those for the United Kingdom and Denmark. The MEI seems to be lower in least-favoured regions. This could be because of a lower endowment infrastructure, use of less sophisticated equipment, a lower level of skilled labour, and so on. It could also, however, be due to inappropriate microeconomic policies that hamper efficient resource allocation.

Table E.2 gives the mechanical results of the computations following the methods set out above. In order to make possible a one percentage point additional increase in GDP, gross investment would on these assumptions need to rise in the least-favoured regions of the Community by between 55 and 76 billion ECUs, according to the method considered.

It should be emphasized that this exercise produces only indications of orders of magnitude, which, given unstable data bases and the restrictive

[1] For the weak regions in Spain the MEI is taken to be identical to that of Portugal; for the south of Italy somewhere between those of Portugal and Greece; for the affected regions in the United Kingdom half the (rather high) national figure is used; for Belgium and France the MEI is assumed to be at Italy's levels in Method 2; for the Netherlands a long-term minimum MEI of 0.12 is retained.

Economic growth and investment

Two methods have been considered to establish the link between economic growth and investment:

1. The neo-classical, balanced model of Solow, based on the following relation:

$$\frac{\dot{Q}}{Q} = \frac{\dot{K}}{K} = \frac{I}{K}$$

where Q is output, K is capital stock, and I is net investment, a model which has not been retained because of difficulties, *inter alia*, of measuring the capital stock:

2. Another method, based on the following relation:

$$\frac{\dot{Q}}{Q} = \frac{\dot{Q}}{I} \times \frac{I}{Q}$$

which states that the growth rate can be split into two parts:

(a) the marginal efficiency of investment (MEI), i.e. the ratio of the variation in output to net investment.
(b) The ratio of net investment to output (GDP).

If, for example, the marginal efficiency of investment is 0.25, an additional increase in growth of 1 percentage point will necessitate an increase in the net investment ratio of 4 percentage points.

This method is based on several assumptions:

(a) Constant technological progress in the period for which the marginal efficiency of investment is estimated.
(b) Invariance of the rate of capacity utilization.
(c) No change in the time of utilization of equipment.
(d) No lag for adjustment: output capacity increases as soon as the investment is made.

As the computational exercise is purely mechanical, this method can only give broad order of magnitude. Moreover, the timing of adjustment in the relation between growth and investment is ignored.

theoretical assumptions, could be quite different if the hypotheses are changed. In particular, the marginal efficiency of investment need not be considered unchangeable. On the contrary, in the low-income countries of the Community, the apparent marginal efficiency of investment is low. From a policy point of view (not pursued in this annex), it may be as important to improve the efficiency of investment as to increase its volume.

TABLE E.1 Estimated trend values of the marginal efficiency of investment

Member State	Method 1	Method 2
Portugal	0.17	—
Greece	0.14	—
Ireland	0.14	—
Spain	0.25	0.17
Italy	0.20	0.15
Belgium	0.18	0.15
United Kingdom	0.40	0.20
Netherlands	0.15	0.12
France	0.19	0.15
Germany	0.25	—
Denmark	0.27	—
Luxemburg	0.25	—
EUR-12	0.27	—

TABLE E.2 Increase in capital formation, possibly to be associated with an increase of one percentage point in GDP growth in the less-favoured regions (billion ECUs 1987)

Member State[a]		Net fixed capital formation		Gross fixed capital formation (without housing)	
		Method 1	Method 2	Method 1	Method 2
Portugal	(100%)	1.8	1.8	3.0	3.0
Greece	(100%)	2.8	2.8	4.7	4.7
Ireland	(100%)	2.0	2.0	2.6	2.6
Spain	(50%)	3.6	5.4	6.0	9.0
Italy	(35%)	7.0	9.4	11.6	15.5
Belgium	(20%)	1.1	1.3	2.2	2.6
United Kingdom	(30%)	3.9	7.8	10.3	20.7
Netherlands	(10%)	1.0	1.2	1.5	1.9
France	(20%)	7.1	9.0	12.8	16.2
TOTAL		30.3	40.7	54.7	76.2

[a]Figures in parentheses indicate the percentages of the country's population covered in the calculation, this representing in broad terms the regions with severest economic problems in the country concerned.

Other estimates are available for basic *infrastructure* equipment which are of greater immediate need for the least-favoured regions. Basic infrastructure expenditure (transport, communications, energy, and education) represents about 4 per cent of Community GDP. On the assumption that the average life of such investments is about twenty-five years, the stock of this type of capital

TABLE E.3 Basic infrastructure needs in the least-favoured regions

	Level of endowment hypothesis 1985[a] (EUR 12 = 100)	Gap to index 80 (ECU/capita)	Population 1985 (millions)	10-year total (billion ECU)
Portugal	40	4,000	10.2	40.8
Greece	50	3,000	10.0	30.0
Spain	60	2,000	17.3	34.6
Ireland	60	2,000	3.6	7.2
Italy	60	2,000	20.3	40.6
TOTAL	—	—	—	153.2

[a]Based on data from the study carried out for the Commission by D. Biehl *et al.*, *Die Infrastrukturausstattung der Regionen in der erweiterten Gemeinschaft: Datensammlung und erst Analyse.* Frankfurt, 1986.

in the EC can be estimated to be equal to annual GDP, i.e. 10,000 ECUs per capita (1985).

If over a ten year time period the level of these types of infrastructure in the less-favoured regions were to rise to 80 per cent of the present EC average, the additional expenditure for basic infrastructure might reach 15 billion ECUs per year in the less-favoured regions, (Table E.3), which roughly implies a doubling of the present expenditure.

It is very difficult to establish an inventory of the needs for *basic infrastructure* in the least-favoured regions according to different categories. From the regional development programmes submitted to the Commission for 1986–90 it appears that great priority is given to transport infrastructure (mainly roads), hydraulic works (including electric power stations), educational infrastructure, and to some extent telecommunications, most of which, if accelerated, could be realized within five years.

The main elements based on the Community transport infrastructure progamme and the above-mentioned regional development programmes, are listed in Table E.4.

Detailed figures for other roads, rivers and canals, ports and airport equipment are not available. Total annual outlays required for priority roads and railway infrastructure might be estimated at 3 billion ECUs. It is likely that the needs for total transport infrastructure are well over 6 billion ECU per annum in the least-favoured regions of the EC.

As regards *telecommunications*, estimates have been prepared in a study for the STAR programme.[2] The investment programme for the Mezzogiorno has been estimated at 2,400 million ECUs for the period 1985–90. Applying the

[2] The STAR programme (Services de Télécommunications Avancées dans les Régions) adopted by the Council on 27 October 1986 provides for the installations of modern telecommunications equipment and for aid measures to promote advanced services in the peripheral regions of the EC. The 5-year allocation on the European Regional Fund budget is 780 million ECUs.

TABLE E.4   Transport infrastructure investments

	Length (km)	Estimated cost[a] (million ECUs)
ROADS		
Portugal		
Lisbon–Porto–Spanish border	440	
Porto–Bragança	250	
Aveiro–Vilar Formoso	230	
Lisbon–Faro–Vila Real	280	
Total	1,200	1,500
Spain		
Express road network[b]	3,500	7,000
Greece		
Athens–Saloniki	520	
Athens–Corinth	80	
Igoumenitsa–Volos	300	
Saloniki–Turkish border	440	
Corinth–Kalamata	290	
Total	1,630	3,300
Ireland		
Belfast–Dublin–Cork	450	
Galway–Dublin	220	
Total	670	1,300
Italy	—[c]	
TOTAL	± 7,000	± 13,000
RAILWAYS		
Portugal		
Lisbon–Porto	290	
Coimbra–Spanish border	210	
Lisbon–Madrid	240	
Spain		
Madrid–Seville (1/2)	270	
Madrid–Burgos (1/2)	120	
Burgos–La Coruna (1/3)	160	
Madrid–Zaragossa (1/3)	110	
Zaragossa–Vitoria (1/2)	110	
Zaragossa–Barcelona	290	
Barcelona–Valencia	120	
Total	1,580	850
Italy		
Messina–Catania	90	50
Greece		
Saloniki–Athens–Kalamata	870	500
TOTAL	± 3,300	1,800

[a]Taking into account finished sections. The cost of building a highway in average geographic conditions may be roughly estimated to be 3–4 million ECUs per kilometre; for an expressway 2–3 million ECUs per kilometre. The cost of improving a road network may vary considerably, depending on circumstances.
[b]*Plan General de Carreteras, 1984–1991*.
[c]Main road infrastructure is considered to be sufficient in the south of Italy.

ratio per capita to the other least-favoured regions, the need for telecommunications infrastructure in those regions can be estimated at 6,000 million ECUs, or 1,200 million ECUs per annum.

As regards *hydraulic infrastructure*, in southern Europe the availability of water in sufficient quantity on a regular basis is of paramount importance, not only for agricultural use (irrigation), but also for industrial and domestic use. Annual expenditure for dams, electric power stations, pipes, and so on can be estimated (according to the regional development programmes) at 2.6 billion ECUs. In the Mezzogiorno, Special Projects 14 (Puglia/Campania) and 23 (practically the whole south of Italy) have absorbed about 1 billion ECUs per annum.

It has not been possible to estimate costs for *other infrastructure* equipment such as industrial estates, sewerage, power stations, oil and gas pipelines, and so on.

Likewise, it has not been possible to estimate at a comparable level of detail the infrastructure investment needs of declining industrial regions. Generally speaking, it seems that they are not too badly equipped in basic infrastructure although the quality could often be improved.

In order to develop the economy, both the least-favoured and declining industrial regions need not only physical but human capital as well. As far as *general education* is concerned, it appears that Portugal has a remarkably low level.[3] If this country were to improve its enrolment rate for secondary education up to 80 per cent of the Community level, the number of students would have to increase by 150,000 to a total of 550,000 in 1992. On the assumption that the (current and capital) cost of education is 1,000 ECUs per person,[4] total average annual cost can be estimated at 90 million ECUs, on the assumption of an annual average increase of 30,000 students up to 1992.[5]

In the field of *professional training*, there are important differences between the northern and the southern countries in the EC, both in structure and expenditure. In the least-favoured regions, total unemployment, including underemployment in agriculture, can be estimated at 5 million in 1992 (taking into account an annual net increase of the labour force of 1 per cent). On the assumption that 1 million persons have to be trained (or retrained) annually at a cost of 3,000 ECUs per person, total annual outlays for the least-favoured regions can be estimated at 3 billion ECUs, whereas at the present time they hardly reach 1 billion ECUs. Professional training in these countries

[3] The percentage of eligible pupils in secondary education (scholarization rate) ($\pm$1983) was as follows: Spain 89%, Greece 85%, Ireland 79%, Italy 74%, Portugal 47%. The figure for EUR 12 was 81%.

[4] Estimated on the basis of EUROSTAT, *Education and Training*, 1985.

[5] It should be noted that if 25,000 educated young people emigrate every year (as seems to be the case currently in Ireland), the total net loss in human capital can be estimated at $25,000 \times 5,000 = 125$ m ECUs per year (on the assumption that secondary education takes 5 years).

and regions has also to be better adjusted to real needs. Corresponding estimates for the declining regions could not be made.

The needs for increased *productive investment* may alternatively be estimated in relation to employment objectives. For the least-favoured regions a possible objective could be to reduce the estimated 5 million unemployed to 2.5 million in 1992. If 1 million jobs might be induced through accelerated infrastructure works, a further 1.5 million might be created through direct productive investment. On the assumption that in those countries and regions, one job requires 50,000 ECUs of investment[6] the total amount would be 50,000 × 1.5 million = 75 billion ECUs in a five-year period, or 15 billion ECUs per annum. If, in order to induce these investments, a grant of 40 per cent were offered, this would mean a public expenditure of 6 billion ECUs. Corresponding estimates for declining industrial regions have not been made.

3. Conclusion

The foregoing has assembled a number of very roughly estimated elements of quantification of the increased investment that might be associated with faster economic growth in the less-favoured regions of the Community. These estimates are intended to give some points of reference in relation to the scale of operations of the structural funds of the Community budget and of the loan-financing activities of the Community. Such estimates cannot be taken to imply any particular judgement about the likely rate of return from such investments, and this criterion could in practice need to dominate decisions to fund investment projects and programmes. Moreover, optimality computations relating to the most appropriate projects could change the figures significantly.

---

[6] Estimate based on data from projects for direct productive investment submitted for Regional Fund assistance in 1985.

TABLE E.5 Main indicators for the regions of the Community

RANK	Region	Country	GDP/capita current PPP 1985 (EUR-12 = 100)	Unemployment rate 1986	Population 1985 Total (million)	Population 1985 Cumulative % share
1	Thrakis	GR	43.2	3.6	0.4	0.1
2	Nison Anatolikou Egeou	GR	46.0	6.0	0.3	0.2
3	Extremadura	ESP	46.6	28.6	1.1	0.6
4	Ipirou	GR	47.1	5.0	0.4	0.7
5	Calabria	I	54.4	14.4	2.1	1.4
6	Portugal	POR	54.6	8.7	9.6	4.3
7	Kritis	GR	54.7	4.0	0.5	4.5
8	Thessalias	GR	55.4	8.4	0.7	4.7
9	Kent. ke Dit. Makedonias	GR	56.3	5.8	1.7	5.2
10	Anatolikis Makedonias	GR	57.3	5.6	0.4	5.4
11	Andalucia	ESP	58.3	30.2	6.7	7.4
12	Pelop. & Dit. Ster. Ell.	GR	58.8	5.5	1.3	7.8
13	Anat. Stereas ke Nison	GR	61.4	10.2	4.2	9.2
14	Castilla Mancha	ESP	62.2	15.7	1.7	9.7
15	Sicilia	I	63.0	13.7	5.1	11.2
16	Campania	I	63.4	15.4	5.6	13.0
17	Puglia	I	64.7	13.3	4.0	14.2
18	Basilicata	I	64.7	18.5	0.6	14.4
19	Galicia	ESP	65.4	14.0	2.9	15.3
20	Molise	I	67.8	7.7	0.3	15.4
21	Sardegna	I	68.1	19.3	1.6	15.9
22	Ireland	IRL	69.5	18.7	3.6	17.0
23	Castilla Leon	ESP	70.7	18.2	2.6	17.8
24	Murcia	ESP	70.9	18.4	1.0	18.2

25	Corse	F	73.0	12.5	0.2	18.2
26	Canarias	ESP	73.5	27.3	1.4	18.7
27	Abruzzi	I	74.3	10.5	1.2	19.1
28	Comm. Valenciana	ESP	76.3	19.8	3.8	20.2
29	Cantabria	ESP	78.2	17.9	0.5	20.4
30	Luxembourg (B)	B	78.9	9.8	0.2	20.5
31	Asturias	ESP	78.9	18.9	1.1	20.8
32	Lueneburg	I	79.3	8.0	1.5	21.3
33	Hainaut	B	80.9	14.2	1.3	21.7
34	Namur prov.	B	80.9	11.5	0.4	21.8
35	Limousin	F	81.4	8.9	0.7	22.0
36	Aragon	ESP	81.8	16.7	1.2	22.4
37	Friesland	NL	82.4	10.7	0.6	22.6
38	Languedoc-Roussillon	F	83.6	13.9	2.0	23.2
39	Poitou-Charentes	F	84.8	11.9	1.6	23.7
40	Salop, Staffordshire	UK	85.7	11.2	1.4	24.1
41	Umbria	I	87.3	11.3	0.8	24.4
42	Auvergne	F	88.1	9.6	1.3	24.8
43	Gelderland	NL	88.2	10.2	1.9	25.4
44	Bretagne	F	88.7	11.0	2.8	26.3
45	Limburg (N)	NL	88.9	11.2	1.1	26.6
46	Humberside	UK	89.0	14.1	0.8	26.9
47	Heref. & Worc., Warw.sh.	UK	89.3	10.2	1.1	27.2
48	Navarra	ESP	89.5	17.9	0.5	27.4
49	Northern Ireland	UK	89.7	18.7	1.6	27.9
50	Kent	UK	89.8	9.6	1.5	28.3
51	Oost-Vlaanderen	B	89.8	8.1	1.3	28.7
52	Trier	D	90.3	7.5	0.5	28.9
53	Marche	I	90.5	6.5	1.4	29.3
54	Overijssel	NL	90.8	9.9	1.0	29.7
55	Limburg (B)	B	90.9	13.0	0.7	29.9

TABLE E.5   (*continued*)

RANK	Region	Country	GDP/capita current PPP 1985 (EUR-12 = 100)	Unemployment rate 1986	Population 1985 Total (million)	Population 1985 Cumulative % share
56	Madrid	ESP	91.1	20.5	4.9	31.4
57	Cornwall, Devon	UK	91.3	11.8	1.4	31.8
58	Oberpfalz	D	91.9	6.9	1.0	32.1
59	Rioja	ESP	92.0	16.6	0.3	32.2
60	South Yorkshire	UK	92.1	16.5	1.3	32.6
61	Basse-Normandie	F	92.1	10.2	1.4	33.1
62	Koblenz	D	92.3	6.7	1.4	33.5
63	Cataluna	ESP	92.9	21.6	6.0	35.4
64	Nord-Pas-de-Calais	F	93.0	12.9	4.0	36.6
65	West Yorkshire	UK	93.1	12.3	2.1	37.2
66	Essex	UK	93.3	8.7	1.5	37.7
67	Midi-Pyrénées	F	93.4	9.0	2.4	38.4
68	Niederbayern	D	93.7	5.5	1.0	38.7
69	Lincolnshire	UK	94.0	11.5	0.6	38.9
70	Giessen	D	94.5	5.5	1.0	39.2
71	Veneto	I	94.6	7.1	4.4	40.6
72	Cleveland, Durham	UK	94.6	17.6	1.2	40.9
73	Weser-Ems	D	95.2	10.1	2.1	41.6
74	Pays Vasco	ESP	95.6	24.6	2.2	42.3
75	Pays de la Loire	F	95.6	11.1	3.0	43.2
76	Northumber., Tyne & Wear	UK	96.3	17.4	1.4	43.6
77	Unterfranken	D	96.6	5.0	1.2	44.0
78	Picardie	F	96.6	10.4	1.8	44.6
79	Bourgogne	F	96.7	10.3	1.6	45.1

80	North Yorkshire	UK	96.7	8.6	0.7	45.3
81	Noord-Brabant	NL	96.8	9.4	2.1	46.0
82	Hampshire, Isle of Wight	UK	97.0	8.3	1.6	46.5
83	Schleswig-Holstein	D	97.0	8.4	2.6	47.3
84	Lazio	I	97.4	9.9	5.1	48.9
85	Baleares	ESP	97.5	13.6	0.7	49.1
86	Dum. & Gal., Strathclyde	UK	97.6	16.7	2.5	49.8
87	Dorset, Somerset	UK	97.7	8.8	1.1	50.2
88	Franche-Comté	F	98.0	9.6	1.1	50.5
89	Liège prov.	B	98.8	12.7	1.0	50.8
90	Centre	F	98.9	9.4	2.3	51.5
91	Merseyside	UK	99.2	19.1	1.5	52.0
92	Lorraine	F	99.5	11.1	2.3	52.7
93	West-Vlaanderen	B	99.7	7.2	1.1	53.1
94	East Anglia	UK	99.7	9.0	2.0	53.7
95	E. Sus., Surrey, W. Sus.	UK	100.1	6.2	2.4	54.4
96	Trentino-Alto Adige	I	100.3	6.4	0.9	54.7
97	Muenster	D	101.4	10.1	2.4	55.4
98	West Midlands County	UK	101.5	16.3	2.6	56.3
99	Gwent, M.S.W. Glamorg.	UK	101.6	14.7	1.7	56.8
100	Lancashire	UK	102.2	12.3	1.4	57.2
101	Aquitaine	F	102.3	10.8	2.7	58.1
102	Berk.sh., Buck.sh., Oxf.sh.	UK	102.7	6.1	1.9	58.7
103	Clwy, Dyfe, Gwyn, Powy	UK	102.8	14.0	1.1	59.0
104	Friuli-Venezia Giulia	I	102.8	8.2	1.2	59.4
105	Utrecht	NL	103.0	8.0	0.9	59.7
106	Toscana	I	103.1	8.6	3.6	60.8
107	Kassel	D	103.1	7.2	1.2	61.2
108	Provence-Alpes-C d'Azur	F	103.4	12.9	4.0	62.4
109	Bor, Cen, Fif, Lot, Tay	UK	103.8	13.0	1.8	63.0
110	Zeeland	NL	104.2	6.5	0.4	63.1

TABLE E.5 *(continued)*

RANK	Region	Country	GDP/capita current PPP 1985 (EUR-12=100)	Unemployment rate 1986	Population 1985 Total (million)	Cumulative % share
111	Ost for Storebaelt	DK	104.3	7.8	0.6	63.3
112	Leices.sh., Northamp.sh.	UK	104.4	9.2	1.4	63.7
113	Derbysh., Nottinghamsh.	UK	104.5	11.7	1.9	64.3
114	Champagne-Ardennes	F	104.9	12.6	1.4	64.7
115	Oberfranken	D	105.2	6.0	1.0	65.1
116	Schwaben	D	106.5	4.6	1.5	65.5
117	Avon, Glou.sh., Wiltsh.	UK	106.6	8.9	2.0	66.2
118	Detmold	D	106.7	8.1	1.8	66.7
119	Saarland	D	107.2	10.7	1.0	67.0
120	Arnsberg	D	107.4	9.9	3.6	68.2
121	Bedfordsh., Hertfordsh.	UK	108.2	6.9	1.5	68.6
122	Braunschweig	D	108.4	8.7	1.6	69.1
123	Greater Manchester	UK	108.5	14.0	2.6	69.9
124	Freiburg	D	109.0	4.5	1.9	70.5
125	Drenthe	NL	109.0	9.1	0.4	70.6
126	Tuebingen	D	109.1	3.8	1.5	71.1
127	Piemonte	I	110.6	8.3	4.4	72.5
128	Cumbria	UK	111.4	10.5	0.5	72.6
129	Vest for Storebaelt	DK	111.6	6.8	2.8	73.5
130	Highlands, Islands	UK	112.3	13.8	0.3	73.6
131	Hannover	D	112.4	8.9	2.0	74.2
132	Emilia-Romagna	I	115.7	7.2	4.0	75.5
133	Koeln	D	116.6	8.3	3.9	76.7
134	Rhone-Alpes	F	116.6	8.2	5.1	78.3

135	Haute-Normandie	F	117.0	12.8	1.7	78.8
136	Cheshire	UK	117.1	11.8	0.9	79.1
137	Liguria	I	117.6	7.9	1.8	79.6
138	Alsace	F	118.0	7.1	1.6	80.1
139	Rheinhessen-Pfalz	D	118.5	6.4	1.8	80.7
140	Zuid-Holland	NL	119.0	8.8	3.2	81.7
141	Lombardia	I	119.0	6.7	8.9	84.4
142	Brabant	B	121.3	9.2	2.2	85.1
143	Noord-Holland	NL	121.4	10.6	2.3	85.9
144	Mittelfranken	D	125.4	5.1	1.5	86.3
145	Karlsruhe	D	127.9	4.9	2.4	87.1
146	Grampian	UK	128.6	8.2	0.5	87.2
147	Duesseldorf	D	129.6	9.1	5.1	88.8
148	Antwerpen prov.	B	130.8	9.5	1.6	89.3
149	Luxemburg (G.D.)	L	131.4	2.5	0.4	89.4
150	Stuttgart	D	135.1	3.3	3.4	90.5
151	Valle d'Aosta	I	137.0	4.6	0.1	90.5
152	Oberbayern	D	142.7	4.6	3.7	91.7
153	Hovedstadsregionen	DK	142.9	5.5	1.7	92.2
154	Berlin (West)	D	144.4	8.5	1.8	92.8
155	Bremen	D	148.7	13.2	0.7	93.0
156	Darmstadt	D	150.4	4.7	3.4	94.0
157	Greater London	UK	155.1	11.6	6.8	96.1
158	Ile de France	F	159.4	8.1	10.2	99.3
159	Hamburg	D	195.5	11.4	1.6	99.8
160	Groningen	NL	237.4	13.2	0.6	100.0

Source: European Commission, Directorate General for Regional Policy.
Notes: Portugal is included at country level; data refer to continental Portugal.
Community averages: GDP/capita (PPP) 1985 = 12189.
Comparable unemployment rate 1986 = 10.8.

Annexes

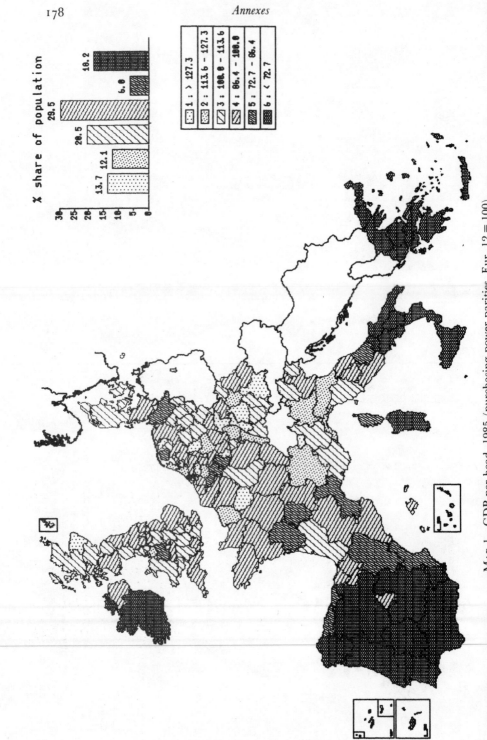

MAP 1 GDP per head, 1985 (purchasing power parities, Eur. 12 = 100)

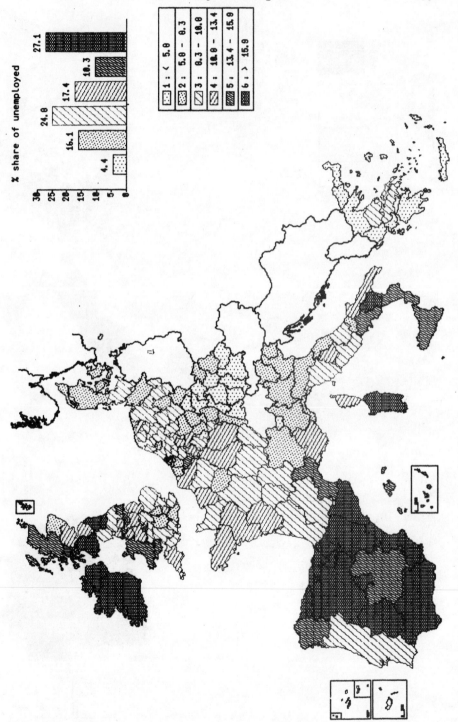

Map 2 Unemployment rates, 1986 (percentages)

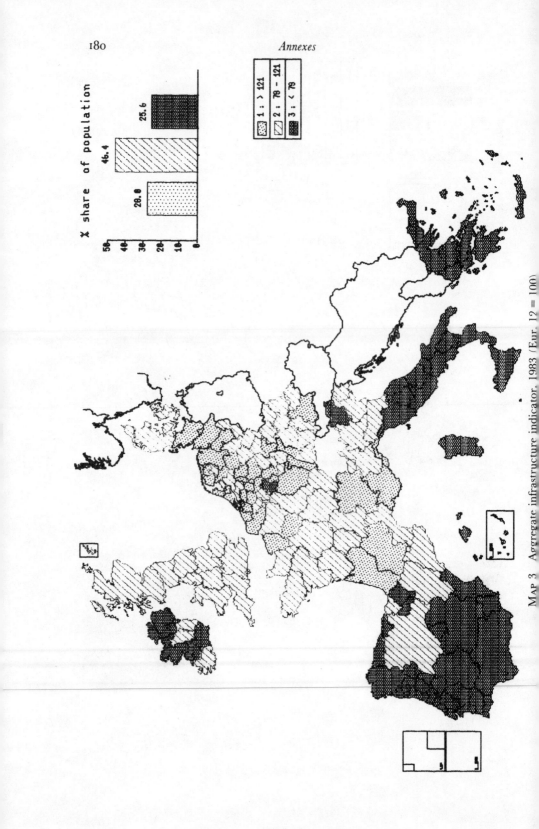

MAP 3   Aggregate infrastructure indicator, 1983 (Eur. 12 = 100)

Index